SCENES
FROM
THE RAMAYAN

SCENES
FROM
THE RAMAYAN

BY

RALPH T. H. GRIFFITH, M. A.

GYAN

Published by

Gyan Publishing House
5, Ansari Road
Daryaganj, New Delhi-110002
Phone: 011-47034999, 9811692060
E-mail: books@gyanbooks.com

Distribution Network
gyanbooks.com
India, USA, Canada, UK, Australia, France

ISBN : 978-81-212-2586-1 (HB)
First Published, 1870

2nd Impression 2021

Printed at: Gyan Press, Delhi.

Scenes from the Ramayan
Author: Ralph T. H. Griffith

SCENES

FROM

THE RAMAYAN

BY

RALPH T. H. GRIFFITH, M.A.

REPRINTED AND PUBLISHED BY

PANINI OFFICE, BAHADURGANJ, ALLAHABAD

1912

"The history and the philosophy of antiquity are invaluable, and could ill be spared; but its poetry is what makes the ancient world near of kin to us, and is that by which we feel that the men of old were bone of our bone and flesh of our flesh. The poetry of a race is what redeems it from perishing as a race, and immortalizes not only the individual poet, but the men who first loved his song and were gladdened by it. This is what binds together the hearts of the ancient and modern worlds."

—*Saturday Review.*

CONTENTS.

PREFACE

There are two recensions of the Ramayana, one belonging to Benares and the North-West of India, the other to Bengal proper. Two books out of the seven of which the latter consists, were published with an English prose translation in 1806 and 1810 by Carey and Marshman, the venerable Missionaries of Serampore. Two books of the Benares recension, with an excellent Latin translation of the first book and part of the second, were published in 1829 by Augustus William Von Schlegal. A magnificent edition of the Bengal recension, with an accurate and elegant translation into Italian, has since been brought out, under royal auspices, by Signor Gorresio of Turin, and a French translation of this edition has been published by M. Hippolyte Fauche. There is an excellent article on the Ramayana in the Westminster Review, Vol L., and another full of interesting information on the same subject in the 45th Number of the Calcutta Review. Professor Williams's "Indian Epic Poetry" gives a full analysis of the Poem with several metrical specimens and Mrs. Speir in "Life in Ancient India," and Mlle. Clarisse Bader in "La Femme dans L'Inde Antique" have written lovingly and gracefully upon the great work of

Valmiki. To these authorities (and to Mr. Talboys Wheeler's second volume of his History of India) the reader is referred for the results of European criticism upon the poem and for the opinions formed of it in the West by those who have become acquainted with the great poem of the Hindus either in the original or by means of translation. Here, instead of an introduction of my own, I offer what I think will be more interesting, some remarks by Baboo Pramadadas Mittra, an orthodox Hindu, formerly my pupil and now my esteemed colleague.

"The Ramayana is the oldest and most glorious poem of India, and its author, the saint Valmiki, who is consequently called *Adi-kavi* or the Father of poetry, is held in the greatest veneration. "I adore that *kokila* —Valmiki, who mounted on the branch of poesy, warbles in honeyed accents " 'Rama' and 'Rama' and 'Rama' again"—this is a literal rendering of the stanza of salutation, composed by an unknown author, which prefaces every manuscript of the poem and genuinely breathes the feelings with which the Hindu regards this holy bard. The account given in the beginning of the poem, of the incidents which led to its composition beautifully harmonizes with the main composition and touchingly shows how exquisitely tender and pure was that saintly heart which breathed forth a poem unrivalled perhaps in the world for its pathos and moral purity. One day the saint accompanied by his disciple resorted to the holy stream Tamasa and finding the waters pure as the heart of the good asked his disciple to fetch his garment of bark. He put it on, and descended into the stream, performed his ablutions and muttered his prayers. Afterwards while roving amidst the woods situated on the banks of the sacred river, he saw a couple of herons wandering secure. On a sudden the male was shot dead by a fowler and the female tossing herself about in the air, screamed out most pitifully her lamentations. At this act of cruelty, the grief of the holy saint burst forth in the exclamation ;

मा निषाद प्रतिष्ठां त्वमगमः शाश्वतीः समाः ।
यत्क्रौञ्चमिथुनादेकमवधीः काममोहितम् ॥

'Never for endless years, O forester, shalt thou obtain rest, as thou hast killed one of the loving couple of herons.'

He was struck with the rhythm of the sentence he had almost unconsciously uttered ; he brooded over it and the piteous event which called it forth. As he was seated in this mood of meditation and tenderness, Brahma himself the Creator of the world appeared, as it is said, before him, exhorted him to sing the deeds of the glorious hero Rama in the metre into which his tenderness had expressed itself, and inspired him with

[1] Or, to versify in the metre of the original, excepting the rhyme :

No rest for ever-circling years, mayst thou, O forester, obtain,
By whose fell hand this harmless bird, while sporting with his mate, was slain.

the knowledge of his whole history, in all its particulars whether hidden or public, the divine saint Narada having already introduced him to it by a relation of the main events. This account which is now contained in the introductory portion of the poem itself was perhaps originally preserved separately by tradition.

Valmiki, who was contemporary with his hero, began to compose his poem when Rama had ascended his paternal throne, having returned from the woods, with his Sita restored.

To write a criticism on the poetry of the Ramayana nicely discerning and aptly delineating the various beauties is a task requiring an ability far more than I can lay claim to. I will therefore simply express the general feelings which its perusal excites in every Hindu of true sensibility. Nowhere else, I believe, are poetry and morality so charmingly united—each elevating the other—as in the pages of this really holy poem. There are indeed many poetical compositions—nay almost all good poetry is such—as forcibly teach us some moral truths, but the Ramayana is the only poem which inspires our breasts with a love of goodness in the entire sense of the word. We rise from its perusal with a loftier idea of almost all the virtues that can adorn man—of truth, of filial piety, of paternal love, of female chastity and devotion, of a husband's faithfulness and love, of fraternal affection, of meekness, of forgiveness, of fortitude, of universal benevolence. What, for instance, can excite a greater reverence of divine Truth than the perusal of that scene where Dasaratha parts with his beloved son for her sake and at last sacrifices his life for her? What can more impressively teach us filial love than the conduct of Rama giving up his domestic felicity, his kingdom, to preserve his father's vow? Well may the Ramayana challenge the literature of every age and country to produce a poem that can boast of such perfect characters as a Rama and a Sita.

The loftiness of its moral tone, though a high one, is not the only recommendation of the poem. It is true, in several places, it is mere prosaic narration, yet there is an ample profusion in it of true poetry—glowing delineations of human passions, delicate paintings of natural beauties, and magnificent descriptions of battle-scenes."

In the "Scenes" now offered to the public something like a connected story of the hero's adventures is given from his birth to the loss of Sita: * * * *
The "Birth of Rama," I should observe, is not from the Ramayana, but from the Raghuvansa of the later poet Kalidasa.

The chief characteristic of the Ramayana being simplicity, I have not attempted to give my lines a polish which would lessen their resemblance to the original, and I have endeavoured rather to be faithful to the spirit of my author and, if possible, to be readable, than to translate as closely as I might have done.

Most of the pieces now published in a collective form have appeared in the *Pandit*, the Benares College Journal of Sanskrit literature: the "Hermit's Son" is reprinted, with a few alterations, from "Specimens of Old Indian Poetry."

BENARES:
July 17*th*, 1868.

[*The present reprint contains a few more pieces which did not appear in the edition published in 1868. These have been taken from the* PANDIT *for 1868 and 1869.*—THE PUBLISHER.]

AYODHYA[1]

" Nous sommes dans Ayodhya, le séjour des princes de la dynastie solaire. Dasaratha règne. Nous sommes en plein âge d'or, et en lisant les curieuses descriptions de la royale cité, on se fait une haute idée de la civilisation de l'Inde, dans un siècle antérieur à celui de Salomon."—MLLE. CLARISSE BADER, *La Femme dans l'Inde Antique.*

On pleasant Sarju's[2] fertile side
There lies a rich domain,
With countless herds of cattle thronged,
And gay with golden grain.

There, built by Manu,[3] Prince of men,
That saint by all revered,
Ayodhya, famed through every land,
Her stately towers upreared.

Her vast extent, her structures high,
With every beauty deckt,
Like Indra's city,[4] showed the skill
Of godlike architect.

[1] The ruins of the ancient capital of Rama and the Children of the Sun may still be traced in the present Ajudhya, near Fyzabad. Ajudhya is the Jerusalem or Mecca of the Hindus.

[2] The Sarju or Ghagra, anciently called Sarayu, rises in the Himalayas, and after flowing through the province of Oudh falls into the Ganges.

[3] This Manu was the first prince of the Solar dynasty: " First Manu reigned, revered by every sage."—*Raghuvansa*, I. 16.

[4] Indra is the Hindu Jove. The name of his celestial city is Amaravati.

Or, like a bright creation sprung
From limner's magic art,
She seemed too beautiful for stone:
So fair was every part.

Twelve leagues the queenly city lay
Down the broad river's side,
And, guarded well with moat and wall,
The foeman's power defied.

Her ample streets were nobly planned,
And streams of water flowed
To keep the fragrant blossoms fresh,
That strewed her royal road.

There many a princely palace stood,
In line, on level ground;
Her temple, and triumphal arc,
And rampart banner-crowned.

There gilded turrets rose on high
Above the waving green
Of mango-groves and bloomy trees,
And flowery knots between.

On battlement and gilded spire
The pennon streamed in state;
And warders, with the ready bow,
Kept watch at every gate.

She shone a very mine of gems,
The throne of Fortune's Queen:
So many-hued her gay parterres,
So bright her fountains' sheen.

Her pleasure-grounds were filled at eve
With many a happy throng,
And ever echoed with the sound
Of merry feast and song.

For meat and drink of noblest sort
In plenty there were stored:
And all enjoyed their share of wealth,
Nor heaped the miser's hoard.

At morn the blossom-scented air
The clouds of incense stirred,
And blended, with the wreath's perfume,
The sweet fresh smell of curd.

Streamed through her streets, in endless line,
Slow wain and flying car:
Horse, elephant, and merchant train,
And envoys from afar.

Her ample arsenals were filled
With sword, and club, and mace:
And wondrous engines, dealing death,[1]
Within her towers had place.

Nor there unknown the peaceful arts,
That youthful souls entrance,
Of player, ministrel, mime, and bard,
And girls that weave the dance.

[1] The *śatagní*, *i.e.*, *centicide*, or slayer of a hundred, is generally supposed, says Wilson, to be a sort of fire-arms, or the ancient Indian rocket; but it is also described as a stone set round with iron spikes.

There rose to heaven the Veda-chant,
Here blent the lyre and lute:
There rang the stalwart archer's string,
Here softly breathed the flute.

The swiftest horses whirled her cars,
Of noblest form and breed:
Vanayu's[1] mare that mocked the wind,
And Vahli's[2] fiery steed.

There elephants, that once had roamed
On Vindhya's mountains, vied
With monsters from the bosky dells
That shag Himalaya's side.

The best of Brahmans, gathered there,
The flame of worship fed;
And, versed in all the Vedas' lore
Their lives of virtue led.

By penance, charity, and truth,
They kept each sense controlled,
And, giving freely of their store,
Rivalled the saints of old.

Her dames were peerless for the charm
Of figure, voice, and face:
For lovely modesty and truth,
And woman's gentle grace.

[1] The situation of Vanayu is not exactly determined: it seems to have lain to the North-West of India.

[2] Vahli, or Vahlika, is the modern Balkh.

Their husbands, loyal, wise, and kind,
Were heroes in the field,
And sternly battling with the foe,
Could die, but never yield.

The poorest man was richly blest
With knowledge, wit, and health;
Each lived contented with his own,
Nor envied other's wealth.

All scorned to lie: no miser there
His buried silver stored:
The braggart and the boast were shunned,
The slanderous tongue abhorred.

Each kept his high observances,
And loved one faithful spouse;
And troops of happy children crowned,
With fruit, their holy vows.

RAVAN DOOMED.

"Lanka, or Ceylon, had fallen under the dominion of a prince named Ravan, who was a demon of such power that by dint of penance he had extorted from the God Brahma a promise that no immortal should destroy him. Such a promise was as relentless as the Greek Fate, from which Jove himself could not escape; and Ravan, now deeming himself invulnerable, gave up asceticism and tyrannized over the whole of southern India. At length even the Gods in heaven were distressed at the destruction of holiness and oppression of virture consequent upon Ravan's tyrannies; and they called a council in the mansion of Brahma, to consider how the earth could be relieved from such a fiend."—MRS. SPEIR, *Life in Ancient India.*

Thus to the Lord, by whom the worlds were made
The Gods of Heaven in full assembly prayed:
"O Brahma, mighty by thy tendered grace
Fierce Ravan, leader of the giant race,
Torments the Gods, too feeble to withstand
The ceaseless fury of his heavy hand.
From thee well pleased, he gained, in days of old,
That saving gift by which he waxes bold;
And we, obedient to that high behest,
Bear all his outrage, patient and opprest.
He scourges—impious fiend—earth, hell, and sky;
And Indra, lord of Gods, would fain defy.
Mad with thy boon, he vexes in his rage
Fiend, angel, seraph, Brahman, saint, and sage.
From him the sun restrains his wonted glow,

Nor dares the wind upon his face to blow;
And Ocean, necklaced with the wandering wave,
Stills the wild waters till they cease to rave.
O Father, lend us thine avenging aid,
And slay this fiend, for we are sore afraid."

They ceased. Then, pondering in his secret mind,
"One way," He said, "to stay this scourge, I find.
Once, at his prayer, I swore his life to guard
From God and angel, fiend, and heavenly bard:
But the proud giant, in o'erweening scorn,
Recked not of mortal foe, of woman born.
Man, only man, this hideous pest may slay:
None else can take his charmed life away."

When Brahma's speech the Gods and sages heard,
Their fainting souls with hope reviving stirred.
Then, crowned with glory like a mighty flame,
Lord Vishnu timely to the council came:
Shell, mace, and discus in his hands he bore,
And royal raiment, tinged with gold, he wore.
Hailed by the Gods, most glorious to behold,
With shining armlets, forged of burnisht gold,
He rode his eagle through the reverent crowd,
Like the sun borne upon a darksome cloud.
Lost in deep thought he stood by Brahma's side,
While all the Immortals praised his name, and cried

"O Vishnu, Lord divine, thine aid we crave,
Friend of the worlds, the ruined worlds to save.

Divide thy godhead, Lord, and for the sake
Of Gods and men man's nature on thee take[1]
Shrined in the bodies of four children, spring
From the three wives of fair Ayodhya's king :
High rank with saints that godly prince may claim,
And those sweet queens, with Beauty, Grace, and Fame.
Assume man's nature thus, and slay in fight
This common scourge, who laughs at heavenly might :
This giant Ravan who, in senseless pride,
Has, trusting to his own right arm, defied
The hosts of Heaven, and ever plagues with woe
Seraphs and Gods above and saints below.
Crusht are the Blest, who roam throuh Nandan's[2] shade
The saint, the seraph, and the heavenly maid.
We, with the sages, Lord, to thee draw nigh,
And crave thy succour that the fiend may die.
Angel and chorister before thee bow :
Our surest hope, O conquering Lord, art thou.
Arise, O King, regard the world below,
And slay in fight the Gods' tremendous foe."

Thus prayed the Children of the Sky ; the lord
Supreme of Gods, by all the worlds adored,
Thus to the suppliants in answer spake :
" Fear not, ye sons of Heaven, but comfort take ;
Ravan, your terror, by this hand shall fall,
With son and grandson, lord and captain ; all

[1] *Cp. Paradise Lost*, Book III, 281 :—
" Their nature also to thy nature join.
And be thyself man among men on earth. "
[2] Indra's celestial garden.

His friends and counsellors, his kith and kin,
Shall share his ruin as they share his sin.
Thus will I triumph o'er the foe, and then
Dwelling as man among the sons of men,
The while ten thousand seasons roll away,
Will guard the earth with mine imperial sway."

Then nymyh and angel, and the minstrel throng,
With heavenly voices, raised their choral song:[1]
And all the region, filled with music, rang
With lauds to Madhu's[2] victor, while they sang:
"Go forth and fight, and strike the monster dead,
The scourge of saints, immortal Indra's dread;
The fell fiend Ravan, ravener[3] abhorred;
Slay him, and all his race, avenging Lord!
Then turn triumphant to thine home on high,
And reign for ever in the ransomed sky."

[1] *Cp.* Paradise Lost, Book III, 344:—
"No sooner had the Almighty ceased, but all
The multitude of angels, with a shout
Loud as from numbers without number, sweet
As from blest voices, uttering joy, Heaven rung
With jubilee, and loud Hosannas filled
The eternal regions."

[2] Madhu was a Daitya or demon slain by Vishnu.

[3] *Virávayam rávaṇam.* Literally Ravan who causes weeping: both words being formed from the root *ru* (Lat. *raucus, rumor*): from which too comes the English word raven.

For a similar play upon the word, *cp. Paradise Regained*:—
"And saw the *ravens* with their horned beaks
Food to Elijah bringing, even and morn,
Though *ravenous*, taught to abstain from what they brought."

THE BIRTH OF RAMA.

"The scene changes to earth, where Dasaratha, King of Ayodhya, after a life spent in deeds of virtue, finds his years drawing to a close without any heir to defend his old age or succeed to his crown. A holy *rishi*, or saint, reveals to him that he shall obtain his desires, on performing the *Aswamedha*, or sacrifice of a horse, which occupies such a pre-eminent place in the Hindu religious rites. The sacrifice is accordingly performed, and with the promised result. Dasaratha's three wives become the mothers of four sons, all participating in the divine nature of Vishnu; but Rama, the eldest, is Vishnu himself."—*Westminster Review, October* 1848, p. 41.

With costly sacrifice, with praise, and prayer,
Ayodhya's king had claimed from Heaven an heir;
When from the shrine, where burnt the holy flame,
Scaring the priests, a glorious angel came,
With arms that trembled as they scarce could hold
A flood of nectar in a vase of gold:
A weight too vast for even him to bear,
For Vishnu's self, the first of Gods, was there.
With reverent awe the Lord of Kosal's land[1]
Received the nectar from the angel's hand,
As erst Lord Indra from the milky wave
Took the sweet drink that troubled ocean gave.[2]

[1] Kosala was the name of the Kingdom of which Ayodhya was the capital.

[2] The *Amrit*, or nectar of the Indian Gods, buried at the Deluge and recovered at the *Churning of the Ocean*. The story is told in the *Mahábhárata* and translated in *Specimens of old Indian Poetry.*

Soon as the queens had shared that mystic bowl,
Hope, sure and steadfast, filled each lady's soul.
They saw, in dreams, a glorious host who kept
Their watch around them, as they sweetly slept.
They mounted skyward on the feathered king,[1]
Who spread a glory with each golden wing,
And as he shot through plains of ether drew
The cloudy rack to follow where he flew.
Now Lakshmi,[2] with her consort's mystic gem
Sparkling upon her breast, for love of them
Came from the skies, and her own radiant hand
Their slumbering eyelids with a lotus fanned.
Then from their homes on high—their holy hair
Damp from the lucid stream that wanders there—
Came, in a glorious dream, the star-throned Seven,[3]
Whispering softly of the Lord of Heaven.

Proud waxed the monarch, as each happy queen
Told the bright visions that her eyes had seen :
No king, he deemed, with him in bliss could vie ;
No, nor the Father of the earth and sky.

[1] The sacred bird of Vishnu, Garuda by name.

[2] Lakshmi, Goddess of Beauty and Fortune, was the wife of Vishnu. The mystic gem is called Kaustubha

"the best
Of gems, that burns with living light
Upon Lord Vishnu's breast."

[3] The seven great saints who are the stars of the constellation of Ursa Major. "The seven great saints who star the northern sky." —*Birth of the War-God.*

As many a river lends its silver breast
Where the calm image of the moon may rest,
So in the bosom of each lady lay
That God, divided, who is one for aye.
Soon, like the luminous herb, which, ere 'tis night,
Wins from the setting sun a ray of light,[1]
Kausalya[2] gained a child, a lovely star,
To chase the shadow of the night afar:
A babe so bright, that every torch grew dim
In the queen's chamber, when it shone near him.
They named him Rama,[3] for the child shall bring
Eternal joy to all who hail him king.
Then the young mother, languid, pale, and worn,
Looked, as she nursed her babe, her newly born,
Like Ganga by the autumn heat opprest,
With one sweet lotus on her island-breast.
And queen Kaikeyi bare a noble child,
Named Bharat, beautiful, and meek, and mild:
By fond affection and obedience, sent
To be his mother's pride and ornament:
Like gentle modesty that lends new grace
To each dear winning charm of Beauty's face.
Then queen Sumitra, fairest of the fair,
Twin children, Lakshman and Satrughna, bare:
Thus self-control and knowledge spring to light
When fruitful learning is employed aright.

[1] The setting sun, say the Indian poets, deposits a portion of his light with certain plants which emit luminous rays in his absence,

"Like gems, in darkness, issuing rays
They've treasured from the sun that's set."—*Lalla Rookh.*

[2] Kausalya was chief of the three queens of Dasaratha.

[3] Rama is derived from the root *Ram*, to sport, take pleasure.

The babes were born: then sin and sorrow fled,
And joy and virtue reigned supreme instead:
For Vishnu's self disdained not mortal birth,
And heaven came with him as he came to earth.
Once more the regions, where each guardian lord
Had quailed before the giant he abhorred,
Were cheered with breezes pure from dust and stain,
And freed from terror hailed a gentler reign.
The fire was dimmed by cloudy smoke no more,
And the sun shone untroubled as before.
But Ravan's Glory poured her sorrows down
In jewels dropping from the giant's crown;
While drums of triumph beaten in the sky
Woke the king's music to a glad reply;
And the first rite to bless the joyful hour
Was the rich downpour of a fragrant shower
Of blossoms falling, from the heavenly trees,
On the proud monarch's gilded galleries.

Graced with the holy rites, and nursed with care,
As the babes strengthened, fairer and more fair,
So with their growth increased their father's joy—
An elder brother to each darling boy.
Modest by nature, gentle nurture's aid
More modest still the youthful princes made:
Thus, when the sacred oil its influence lends,
In brighter spires the hallowed flame ascends.
With virtues blent in sweet accord to grace
The ancient line of Raghu's[1] sinless race—

[1] Raghu, the great-grandfather of Rama, was one of the most celebrated of the solar dynasty and has given his name to the family.

As all the seasons of the year combine
To deck the garden where the Gods recline—
They loved as brothers in their royal home,
But still in pairs they ever loved to roam.
Rama and Lakshman closer ties allied,
And Bharat wandered by Satrughna's side,
Linkt in eternal love, like wind and fire,
Or the dear moon and sea his foster-sire.[1]
As when, at summer's close, dark clouds arise,
Bringing sweet comfort to men's longing eyes,
So the fair children won the people's hearts
By gentle graces and attractive arts:
Men deemed that Duty, Profit, Love, and Bliss,
Had come incarnate from their world to this.
And with more pride the father's bosom glowed
For the rare virtues and the love they showed,
Than for the pearls, in countless tribute poured
By the four oceans, to delight their lord.

[1] At the *Churning of the Ocean* the moon with other buried treasures was recovered from the Ocean by whom, therefore, it is still regarded with parental affection.

THE HEIR APPARENT.

"Dasaratha now made preparations for the public acknowledgment of Rama as destined to be the next king in regular succession, and as permitted during his father's lifetime to share with him the honours and fatigues of royalty."—MRS. SPEIR, *Life in Ancient India.*

But best and noblest of the noble four,
Good as the God whom all the worlds adore,
Lord of all virtues, by no stain defiled,
The King's chief glory was his eldest child.
For he was gallant, beautiful, and strong,
Void of all envy and the thought of wrong.
With gentle grace to man and child he spoke,
Nor could the churl his harsh reply provoke.
He paid due honour to the good and sage,
Renowned for virtue and revered for age;
And when at eve his warlike task was o'er
He sat and listened to their peaceful lore.
Just, pure, and prudent, full of tender ruth,
The foe of falsehood and the friend of truth;
Kind, slow to anger, prompt at misery's call,
He loved the people and was loved of all.
Proud of the duties of his Warrior race,
His soul was worthy of his princely place,
Resolved to win, by many a glorious deed,
Throned with the Gods in heaven, a priceless meed.

What though Brihaspati[1] might hardly vie
With him in eloquence and quick reply,
None heard the music of his sweet lips flow
In idle wrangling or for empty show.
He shunned no toils that student's life befit,
But learned the Vedas and all Holy Writ;
And e'en eclipsed his father's archer fame,
So swift his arrow and so sure his aim.

Then rose a longing in the monarch's breast:
"O, that the Gods would take me to their rest;
Might I but see, ere yet my course be run,
The hallowed waters poured upon my son:
See in mine age, a worthy heir, mine own
Beloved Rama on Ayodhya's throne."
Then with his friends he counselled that his heir
Should ease his burthen and divide the care.
For, old and worn, he felt that death was nigh,
And dark signs threatened both in earth and sky.
But still he quailed not, for he knew how dear
All held Prince Rama, and this banisht fear.

Forthwith he summoned, for the solemn day,
People and princes near and far away.
They came: and splendid in his king's attire
He looked upon them, as the Eternal Sire,
In all the glory of a God arrayed,
Gazes upon the creatures he has made.

Like heavenly music, very sweet and loud,
Thus spake the monarch to the gathered crowd:

[1] The Preceptor of the Gods.

"Needs not for me, ye noble lords, to show,
How like fond fathers, as fathers, as full well ye know,
The ancient monarchs of our famous line
Have ruled this mighty realm which now is mine.
Their glorious steps forbade my feet to stray,
And I have laboured, with a loving sway,
'Neath the white canopy's imperial shade,[1]
Till strength is vanisht and my health decayed,
To bless my people, if they have been blest,
And now my weary spirit longs for rest;
For many thousand years have o'er me flown,[2]
And many generations round me grown
And past away. No longer can I bear
The ruler's labour and the judge's care,
The royal power and dignity, a weight
Too vast but for the young and temperate.
I long to rest, mine anxious labour done,
And on the throne to set my darling son.
For all the virtues lent to me adorn
Rama my dearest and my eldest born.
Ye have the plan which I have pondered long
Approve it now, or, if ye deem it wrong,
Show, after due consult, a wiser way,
Which I will strive to follow if I may."

[1] The white umbrella was one of the insignia of royalty.

[2] The ancient kings of India enjoyed lives of more than atriarchal length:

"While thus, as Indra reigns above the sky,
He ruled the earth, ten thousand years flew by."
—*Raghuvansa*, X. 1.

He ceased. A murmur of so loud acclaim
From lords and commons in glad answer came,
As when wild peacocks at the rain rejoice,
And hail the big cloud with their jubilant voice.
The general shout from all the people round
Shook the high palace with a storm of sound.
And when the crowd, assembled there, had learned
The will of him who right and gain discerned,
After a brief debate, with one accord,
They spake in answer to their sovereign lord :
" Rest, aged king, and let Prince Rama share
The toil too sore for thee, as Regent Heir :
Our own dear prince so gallant and so strong,
All tongues will bless him as he rides along :
All hearts rejoice above his brow to see
The canopy that long has shaded thee.
Amid the noblest of the world not one
Can match the virtues of thy godlike son.
In him alone all peerless graces blend,
The fearless foeman and the faithful friend ;
Versed in the statutes, kind to all in need,
Quick to encourage every noble deed;
True to his promise, resolute of soul,
Curbing each passion with a firm control;
Kind to the Brahmans skilled in Scripture's page,
The friend of learning and the prop of age.
Matchless on earth with spear and sword and shield,
Lord of the arms which heavenly warriors wield ;
Thine order bids him tame some foeman's pride ;
He comes a victor, Lakshman at his side.

Then from his elephant, or car, he bends
To greet the townsmen as beloved friends:
Asks how each man and child and servant thrives,
How fare our young disciples, babes, and wives,
And like a loving father bids us tell
That Heaven accepts our rites, and all is well.
Long has each matron, long each tender maid,
At morn and eve for Rama's welfare prayed:
And Rama's glories every hour are sung
In town and village by the old and young.
Then grant the prayer, by us this day renewed,
And consecrate our Prince, Lord Rama, lotus-hued."

MANTHARA'S GUILE.

"But this happiness was all destroyed by the intrigues of Dasaratha's second wife, who was jealous of Rama, and determined that her son Bharat should be the future king."—MRS. SPEIR.

High on the palace roof Kaikeyi's maid,
The crook-back Manthara, the town surveyed.
She saw the water sprinkled o'er the street,
And flowery heaps and garlands fresh and sweet:
Saw pennons playing in the scented air,
And busy Brahmans bustling here and there.
From every corner, as around she gazed,
She heard a concert of glad music raised;
While every temple shone with purest white,
That the maid marvelled at the festive sight.
She turned to Rama's nurse, who standing by,
Gazed on the scene with rapture-rolling eye,
And cried, "I pray thee, aged matron, say
Does Rama's mother scatter gifts to-day?
Have the Gods listened to Kausalya's vow,
And made the frugal queen so lavish now?"

The white-robed nurse, with transport uncontrolled,
All the glad story to the damsel told:
"To-morrow's happy light will see," she cried,
"Prince Rama Regent by his father's side."

Down from the roof, high as Kailasa's[1] head,
In furious haste the crook-backt maiden sped:

[1] One of the loftiest peaks of the Himalayas.

Planning accursed guile, her soul aflame,
Where queen Kaikeyi lay asleep, she came.
"Up, queen!" she cried, "unclose thy heedless eyes;
Huge peril threatens thee, awake! arise!
Art thou still sleeping, still too blind to see
The load of misery that crushes thee?
Boast of thy husband's love, and find too late
His vaunted favour but disguises hate.
Ruin to thee and thine, thy lord has planned
To make Prince Rama Regent o'er the land.
In fear and grief and rage thy faithful slave
Has hither fled to warn thee and to save.
Are not my fortunes closely knit with thine?
Thy gain and peril, both, are also mine.
And thou, the scion of a royal race,
Shouldst know the frauds which royal hearts disgrace.
Poor queen, he loves thee not: thy treacherous lord
Can smile upon thee while he bares the sword:
And thy sweet soul, pure from all thought of sin,
Sees not the cruel snares that hem thee in.
Kind flattering words he makes thine empty dower
But queen Kausalya has the wealth and power.
Far from thy side thine own dear son he sends
To live an exile with his mother's friends;
And, every rival thus removed from sight,
He gives to Rama all the royal might.
Alas! deluded lady, thou hast prest
A deadly serpent to thy foolish breast,
Lavishing love on him who works thee woe,
No loving husband but a mortal foe.

Come, rouse thee, mistress, while there yet is time,
Ensure thy safety and prevent the crime.
Up from thy careless ease! awake, and be
The saviour of thy son, thyself, and me."

Up rose Kaikeyi radiant with delight,
Like the calm moon upon the autumn night,
And spoke these words in answer, as she gave,
For the glad news, a necklace to the slave:
"Take this, dear maiden, for thy pains, and say
How can my love thy welcome tale repay.
I joy that Rama shares his father's throne:
I love Kausalya's son e'en as I love mine own."
The handmaid's soul with grief and fury burned;
She cried in anger, as the gift she spurned:
"What! on the sea of whelming ruin tost,
Canst thou rejoice when all but hope is lost?
Heart-sick I am, yet smile to see thy joy
When peril threatens and will soon destroy.
If thou wert wise thou scarce wouldst hail, I ween,
For king, the offspring of a rival queen.
Soon wilt thou stand in menial habit drest,
And move obedient to her high behest.
Yea, thou wilt serve with us who serve thee now,
And see thy child before his brother bow.
Then Rama's wife will triumph, queen of all,
And thy poor daughter be a helpless thrall."

"The virtuous Rama," thus the dame replied,
"From virtue's path will never turn aside.
Obedient, grateful, pure from stain, and true,
As eldest born he only gains his due.

His lords and brethren many a year will share,
Blest in his rule, his kind paternal care:
And when a hundred years have past away,
My son, dear Bharat, will enjoy the sway.
I love Prince Rama as mine own dear son;
I see no fault to stain him, no not one.
Gentle and lowly, good and kind is he,
Meek to his mother, meeker still to me.
What though he rule, there is no cause of fear,
To him his brethren as his soul are dear:
And though in name his father's place he fill
Bharat will share the royal sceptre still."

Kaikeyi ceased: the impatient maiden sighed,
And thus with tears of grief and spite replied:
"Ah queen, what frenzy has assailed thy mind,
And made thee thus to instant danger blind?
Too blind to mark the seas of grief and woe,
That o'er thy head with whelming fury flow.
For after Rama Rama's son will reign,
Nor hope of kingship for thy child remain.
One heir is monarch when a monarch dies,
Else wild confusion in the state would rise:
And be he good or bad, the power will fall
To him, the eldest born, and lord of all.
Know, tender mother, that thy boy must flee,
A wretched outcast, from his home and thee.
For Rama's hand thy darling son will drive
An exile hence, if haply left alive.
Come take the counsel that is wise and good,
And banish Rama to the distant wood.

Then we who serve thee well, a faithful train,
Will hail with joy Prince Bharat's happier reign.
How shall he, worthy of a nobler fate,
From birth the object of his brother's hate,
Poor and despised, his wealthy tyrant's scorn,
Obey the mandates of the elder born ?
Arise, sweet queen, to save thy child, arise !
Prostrate beneath his brother's feet he lies;
Like some young elephant, who, proud to lead
His trooping consorts through the woods to feed,
Meets with a hungry lion in the way
And sinks in death, his ruthless victor's prey."

Then flasht the fury from Kaikeyi's eyes,
As thus she spake with long and burning sighs:
"This day my son upon the throne shall see,
And Rama banisht to the wood shall flee.
But aid me, damsel, and some plan declare
To drive him hence and make my child the heir."
"Hast thou forgotten?" thus the maid replied,
"Or dost thou love thy secret thoughts to hide?
Or dost thou wish, gay queen, to hear me tell
An ancient story which thou knowest well?
Then I will speak: Lady, be thine to hear,
And mark my counsel with attentive ear.
In days of yore the Gods thy husband chose
To aid their arms against their demon foes.
Thou, of thy love, didst follow where he led,
And thou wast near him when he fought and bled.
Thy care preserved him, when in desperate strife
He sank exhausted, and restored his life.

Grateful for this, thy loving husband sware
To grant two boons, thy first and second prayer.
Then come, remind him of his ancient oath,
Recall the promised gifts and claim them both.
For thine own son, thy well-loved Bharat, claim
The right of heirship and the Regent's name,
And pray that Rama in the woods may roam,
Twice seven long years an exile from his home.
Once more attend: the gloomy chamber[1] seek,
Rage in thine eye and tears upon thy cheek;
With robes disordered and dishevelled hair,
Fall on the cold ground and lie prostrate there.
When the king comes, still sad and speechless lie,
Give him no answer, lift not up thine eye.
Well do I know that thou hast ever been,
And more than ever art, his favourite queen.
For thy dear sake he'd dare, O well-loved dame,
To cast his body to the burning flame:
Such death were welcome, but he ne'er will brook
To anger thee or bear thine angry look.
Fain will he offer gems and pearls and gold:
Heed not his gifts: be silent, stern and cold.
Then to his mind those promised boons recall,
And claim them boldly: he will grant thee all.
When he has raised his darling from the floor,
And sworn again to grant as first he swore,

[1] Literally, *the chamber of wrath*, a small, low, dark, unfurnished room, to which, it seems, the wives and ladies of the king used to betake themselves when offended, with a view to work more effectually upon the feelings of their lord.

Then for thy son demand the royal sway,
And drive Prince Rama to the woods away.
Hope, and be bold : king is well inclined,
And this the hour to move his easy mind."

Then queen Kaikeyi, full of joy and pride,
Thus to her maid in gladsome tone replied :
" Good is the plan thy ready wits devise,
Sagest of damsels, true and deep and wise !
Without thy constant care, thy faithful aid,
Unknown to me the king his plot had laid.
The crook-backt race are hideous to the sight,
Deformed, malicious, born for guile and spite :
Far other thou, with features formed to please,
A lovely lotus bending to the breeze.
Thy hump, dear damsel, too, becomes thee well,
For there the arts of noble warriors dwell ;
And when Kausalya's son makes way for mine,
Around that hump a chain of gold shall shine.
Yes, I will deck thee on that happy day
When Rama banisht takes my fears away :
With finest gold these hands thy hump shall deck,
And fling rich pearls around thy graceful neck.
A precious frontlet, wrought with utmost care,
Bound on thy brow, shall make thy face more fair ;
And thou shalt move along in bright attire,
Each woman's envy and each man's desire :
Fair as a lovely Goddess shalt thou be,
And challenge the sweet moon to rival thee."

Her lady's praise with joy the damsel heard,
And thus again with wiles her spirit stirred,
As the queen lay upon her sumptuous bed,
Like sacred fire upon the altar fed :
" Mistress, arise, the glorious plot complete :
Let the king find thee in thy dark retreat.
No prudent builder will the bridge delay
Till the wild waters shall have rolled away."
She ceased. The lady of the glorious eyes
Rose from her couch as Manthara bade her rise ;
And sought the mourner's cell, in beauty's pride
Sure of his love who gave and ne'er denied.
There on the ground, obedient to the girl,
She threw her necklace and each peerless pearl,
And all the lustre to her beauty lent
By sparkling chain and golden ornament.
Like a fair nymph upon the ground she fell ;
And, " Soon," she cried, " thy task will be to tell
That Bharat rules as heir in Rama's stead,
Or that the monarch's darling queen is dead."

DASARATHA'S OATH.

"Unfortunately Dasaratha had once given a promise to Bharat's mother that he would grant any two boons she pleased to ask. The promise had been made in years gone by, when he had been dangerously wounded in battle, and carefully attended by this wife, Kaikeyi; and amongst Hindus a promise was irrevocable, and therefore the wretched King felt compelled to yield, although the first boon required was to banish Rama for a period of fourteen years, and the second to declare Bharat the heir-apparent."—*Life in Ancient India.*

Slow and majestic, as the Lord of Night,[1]
When his full glory fears the Dragon's[2] might,
Glides through the calm fields of the autumn sky,
Where clouds with fleecy skirts are floating by,
So to Kaikeyi's palace, rich and vast,
King Dasaratha in his glory past.
There stalked flamingoes mixt with swans and cranes,
And gorgeous peacocks spread their jewelled trains;
There screamed the parrot in his home of wire,
There breathed the music of the flute and lyre.

[1] The moon, with the Hindus, is masculine.

[2] Rahu, the ascending node, is in mythology a demon with the tail of a dragon whose head was severed from his body by Vishnu but being immortal the head and tail retained their separate existence, and being transferred to the stellar sphere, became the authors of eclipses; the first especially by endeavouring to swallow the sun and moon.

There many a damsel waited in the shade,
Here sat a dwarf, and there a crook-backt maid
Lay in the shadow of the woven bower
Where glowed the Champac[1] and Asoca[2] flower.
There many a porch, above the waving wood,
On ivory columns wrought with silver, stood.
There trees that aye with fruit and blossom glowed
O'er limpid waters hung their tempting load.
Here seats of silver and of gold were placed,
Here cates and viands lured the dainty taste.
Not e'en the Gods who dwell at ease, I ween,
Could boast a brighter home than that fair queen.

With longing eyes the monarch looked around,
But no Kaikeyi in her bower he found;
Yet 'twas the time at which the royal dame
Was ever there to greet him as he came.
Then, moved by love and vext with anxious thought,
News of his darling from her maids he sought.
"My lord," a trembling damsel thus replied,
"The queen in anger to the cell has hied."
Then sick at heart, his senses all astray,
The monarch hastened where the lady lay
Upon the cold bare ground, in mean attire,
While grief consumed her as a burning fire.

[1] A tree that bears yellow flowers of delicious fragrance:
"The maid of India, blest again to hold
In her full lap the Champac's leaves of gold."—*Lalla Rookh.*

[2] The Jonesia Asoca, one of the loveliest trees of India, and perhaps of the whole world.

Prostrate and speechless, lovely and forlorn,
Like a sweet creeper by the roots uptorn,
Or a frail nymph of heaven, or Goddess, hurled
From glorious Swarga[1] to this nether world.

As bends an elephant to heal the smart
Of his mate wounded by a venomed dart;
Soothes her with tender touch, and tries in vain
To check the flowing blood and stay her pain;
So the sad husband tried each kind caress
To still the fury of the queen's distress:
"I know not, darling," thus he spake, with sighs,
To the fair lady of the lotus eyes,
"The sudden cause of all this wrath and woe,
Why thou art angry, why thine eyes o'erflow.
Who has offended thee, or dared to slight
My love, my lady, and my sole delight?
Tell me, my dearest, art thou faint or ill?
I have physicians of unrivalled skill,
One for each varied malady and pain:
Come, speak, Kaikeyi, and be well again.
Wouldst thou for foe or friend have dole or meed?
The guiltless punisht or the guilty freed?
The low exalted or the proud disgraced?
The poor made wealthy or the rich abased?
Tell but thy secret wish, dear love, I pray;
My lords and I thy slightest word obey.
By all the merit that my life has won
I swear, my darling; speak, and it is done.

[1] Indra's Paradise.

The whole broad earth whereon the sunbeams shine,
And all her flocks and corn and gold are mine;
Choose what thou wilt: no bounds shall bar thy choice,
But let me hear again thine own dear voice,
And all thy grief and pain shall pass away
Like hoar frost shrinking from the God of Day."

The queen replied: "No insult has distrest,
No fault of others has enraged my breast.
Come, with a mighty oath thine honour bind
To grant the boon for which my soul has pined."
She ceased. The king, by his great love betrayed,
Leapt, like a roedeer, to the snare she laid.
With a fond smile beneath his darling's head
He placed his hand, and raised her up, and said:
"Hast thou not learnt, my foolish love, till now,
That on this earth there is none dear as thou
To me, save only Rama? By his life
I swear to grant thee what thou wilt, dear wife:
I swear by him most worthy long to live,
Blest with all blessings that the Gods can give,
My peerless boy, pride of mine aged eye,
Whom but one hour to see not, is to die."

"Now hear," she cried, "ye thirty Gods and three,
Witness the oath that he has sworn to me!
Hear it, ye Sun and Moon; thou Ether, hear;
O Night and Day, O World and Space, give ear!
Listen thou Heaven above; attend O Earth,
With visitants of more than mortal birth!

Angel, and demon, and night-wandering shade,
And Household Deities, our present aid;
Each Power and high Intelligence, with all
That think and know, to hear his oath I call.
And now, I pray thee, O my lord and king,
A time ong past to thy remembrance bring,
When Gods and demons met in furious fray,
And I preserved thee on that awful day.
Call to thy mind the guerdon promised then,
And grant my double prayer, O king of men.
If thou refuse to do as thou hast sworn,
Despised by thee I will not live till morn.
This solemn pomp in Rama's name begun,
Grace Bharat with it : consecrate my son ;
And forth to Dandak's distant forest drive
Thy Rama, banisht for nine years and five :
There let him lead a hermit's life, and wear
The deerskin mantle and the matted hair."

Like a poor doe who sees the tigress near,
Lost and amazed and stupified with fear,
He spoke no word, but, sinking on the ground,
Sighed like a serpent by the charmer bound.
At length, when slowly voice and sense returned,
He bent upon the queen fierce eyes that burned
With flashes of intolerable ire,
Eager to scorch her with their furious fire :
" What wrong," he cried, " have I or Rama done,
Scourge of my house, thou fell and wicked one ?
Hast thou the heart to ruin my sweet boy,
And him who loves thee as a son, destroy ?

Ah! woe is me that e'er I made thee mine,
And brought thee home, the ruin of my line,
In name the daughter of a king, in truth
A deadly serpent with a venomed tooth.
Tell me, what fault can I pretend to find
In virtuous Rama, praised by all mankind?
How can I then my darling son forsake?
No, take my life, my royal honours take,
Be either queen from my embraces torn;
But not my Rama, not mine eldest born.
Gazing on him mine aged eyes are glad,
And when I see him not my soul is sad.
The world may live without the sun, the grain
Spring from the earth without the genial rain;
But I without my son should be no more:
Take Rama from me, and my life is o'er.
Banish the thought! thine impious plan forego;
How couldst thou scheme a plot so full of woe?
Canst thou no mercy find, no sorrow feel?
See, with thy feet upon my head, I kneel.
Thou dost not mean it: 'tis a cruel jest
To try the love that warms a father's breast.
Hast thou not oft, when in thy lap he smiled,
Sworn he was dear to thee as thine own child?
Has he not since, to youth and manhood grown,
Most sonlike love and sweet obedience shown?
Never from man or woman have I heard
Against my Rama one accusing word.
His gentle manners, ever soft and kind,
All hearts to him in firm affection bind.

Truthful and just, that noble prince of men
Is loved and honoured by each citizen.
A docile pupil, prompt to succour woe,
Feared by the foeman for his matchless bow,
Faithful and pious, reverent, sincere,
Holy and wise, to all most justly dear:
Canst thou for him thy wicked plot devise,
Good as the Gods, and, as the sages, wise?
No angry word, no harsh reproof, e'er slips
From the fair portal of his gentle lips.
And at thy bidding how can I consent
To curse him with the doom of banishment?
O wife, have mercy! hear my bitter cry,
A poor old weeping man whose death is nigh.
This sea-girt land has treasures rich and rare:
Take all, Kaikeyi, but my Rama spare.
Once more, O queen, my suppliant hands entreat;
Once more my lips are on thy lovely feet:
O save my Rama, save my dearest child,
Nor let me die a wretch dishonoured and defiled."

No thrill of pity through her bosom ran,
As thus again the cruel queen began:
"If thou hast promised and art now forsworn,
How wilt thou keep thine ancient name from scorn?
When gathered kings thy truth and honour praise,
How wilt thou bear thine abject eyes to raise
And answer thus: 'Ah! kings, ye little know;
My queen to whose fond care my life I owe,
Saved by whose sweet love I am living now,
To her I promised and I broke my vow.'

Then will they scorn the king once counted just,
And tread his vaunted honour in the dust.
His flesh and blood the truthful Saivya[1] gave,
And fed the hawk, a suppliant dove to save:
True to his word Alarka gave his eyes,
And gained rich guerdon in the blissful skies.
The furious sea himself his promise keeps,
And ne'er beyond his stated limit sweeps.
Remember all I did for thy dear sake,
And tremble now thy promised word to break.
Thou hopest Rama to the throne to raise,
And with Kausalya live voluptuous days.
But be it truth or falsehood, right or wrong,
I claim thy promise unredeemed so long.
Make Rama Regent, and before thine eyes
This day Kaikeyi drinks the bowl, and dies.
Far better die, than live one day, to see
Obsequious subjects, with no glance on me,
Before my rival, Rama's mother, stand,
And hail her lady with the suppliant hand.
Now by my son and by myself I swear,
No tears shall soften me, no gift or prayer;
This, only this, shall now my soul content:
I claim thine oath and Rama's banishment."

[1] A just and truthful king, who being unwilling to deprive a hawk of his prey or to betray the dove to which he had promised protection, gave his own flesh to the hawk who would accept nothing else instead. The story is told in the *Mahabharata*, in different ways, of more than one king.

THE STEP-MOTHER.

Tho night "long and dreary as a hundred years" which the unhappy king has spent in lamentation and entreaties to the inexorable Kaikeyi is past, and the morning appointed for the consecration of Rama is come. Ramá having been summoned enters the chamber where the king and Kaikeyi are.

Weighed down by woe, with wild despairing mien,
There sat the monarch with the cruel queen.
Then Rama bowed, his royal sire to greet,
And did obeisance at Kaikeyi's feet.
The king with downcast eyes still brimming o'er,
Just murmured, Rama ! and could do no more.
Then sudden fear made even Rama shake,
As though his heedless foot had toucht a snake.
How could he look upon that awful change,
And bear, unmoved, a sight so sad and strange !
A mighty monarch but an hour ago,
Now a poor mourner, weak and wan with woe :
Weeping and groaning, mad with wildering thought,
Like the deep wave-crowned sea to frenzy wrought :
Like the bright sun-god labouring in eclipse,
Or like a holy sage whose heedless lips
Have spoken falsely. Rama's tender breast
Knew for a while the moon-drawn sea's unrest ;
And, pierced with sorrow for his father's sake,
To queen Kaikeyi, reverent, he spake :

" Tell me my fault, or plead for me and win
His pardon, angered by my careless sin.

Why is my father, whom I ever find
Most full of love, so silent and unkind?
To what sharp anguish or what care a prey
Weeps he and sighs and turns his face away?
Say, has some grievous woe, some deadly ill,
Stricken his sons, or consorts dearer still?
Better to die than grieve a loving sire:
Death has no terror like a father's ire.
Surely the source to which he owes his birth
Must to a son be as a God on earth.
Then speak, O lady, speak, that I may know
What sudden grief has changed my father so."

Thus Rama questioned; and the greedy dame
Gave her bold answer, lost to ruth and shame:
"No fault of thine thy father's soul offends;
No deadly stroke upon his house descends.
One wish he fosters, to his heart most dear;
And he would tell thee, but he shrinks in fear.
Thou art so fondly loved, no voice has he
To utter aught but pleasant words to thee.
Then hear his wish, and, as a duteous son,
Look that thy father's will be quickly done.
He, though a king, with most unkingly mind
Like a mean caitiff of the lowest kind,
Would stint the honour and the boon deny
He sware to grant me in the days gone by.
Faith, holy faith, whence all our duties spring,
Should ne'er be slighted by our lord the king.
Not e'en in anger, not for thy dear sake,
May he his oath and plighted promise break.

He will not say what promised boon I seek;
Before thy face he will not, dare not, speak.
Do thou but swear his promise shall not fall
Lost to the ground, and I will tell thee all."

She ceased. Then Rama, with a troubled breast,
These words in answer to the queen addrest:
" Thou needst not utter words like these to me:
To do his will my highest joy must be.
To feed the flames my body I will throw;
Drink deadly poison, if his will be so;
Plunge in the tide if he would have it done,
My sire, my master, and my king in one.
Then speak, O lady; with no doubting heart
The secret longing of my sire impart.
I swear obedience: let my word suffice,
For 'tis not Rama's wont to promise twice."

Then spoke Kaikeyi to the noble youth,
Undaunted champion of the rights of truth:
" When the Gods, aided by thy father's might,
Waged with the fiends, of yore, their furious fight,
Wounded by many a dart the monarch fell,
And I preserved the life I loved so well.
Restored by me to health and strength, he sware
To grant two boons, the guerdon of my care,
And these, at length, I crave this day may be
The throne for Bharat and the woods for thee.
Now if his honour in thine eyes be dear,
Keep his fair fame from stain of falsehood clear.
Go to the distant wilderness, and wear
The hermit's mantle and the matted hair.

Nine years and five in the wild forest stay,
That Bharat may be lord, ordained to-day;
And then this land, rich in each precious thing,
Steed, car, and elephant, shall hail him King.
Moved with great pity for thy mournful case,
Thy father cannot look upon thy face.
Come, noble prince, his darling honour save,
And, firm in faith, observe the oath he gave."

The hero answered, tranquil and sedate,
That cruel speech, fell as the doom of fate:
"Fear not, O lady, but thy wish obtain:
My father's faith shall ne'er be pledged in vain.
With hermit's mantle and with matted hair
Forth to the woods, an exile, will I fare.
One thing alone, O queen, I fain would learn,
Why is my lord the king to-day so stern?
Why is he now so silent and so cold,
Without one smile to greet me, as of old?
My greatest joy is ever to fulfil
My king, my master, and my father's will;
One only care torments my anxious breast,
Why his own lips have not his will exprest;
Why could he not himself to me make known
His choice of Bharat for the royal throne.
To Bharat's hand I gladly would resign
My bride, my life, my gold and all that's mine.
Unaskt, most freely would I give him all:
How much more gladly at my father's call!
How much more gladly when the gift may free
His fame from blemish and give joy to thee!

Let swiftest heralds, ordered by the king,
Home from thy brother's house thy Bharat bring.
To judge my father's words I will not stay,
But seek the forest ere the close of day;
There live, a banisht man, four years and ten,
Keeping the promise of the king of men."

"'Tis well," she answered. "Let the herald speed,
Carried by coursers of the fleetest breed,
And bring my Bharat home. Methinks that thou
Wilt brook no tarrying nor linger now.
And if the king, o'erwhelmed with shame, could find
No tongue to tell thee, bear not this in mind.
But, best of youths, until thou hence art fled,
Thy sire will neither bathe nor call for bread."

"Woe! woe!" the monarch murmured, with a groan,
Deep 'neath the waves of whelming anguish thrown;
Then in exceeding grief he swooned away,
And on the gold-wrought couch all senseless lay.
Then Rama raised him, while Kaikeyi's tongue
Still urged him, like a horse by lashes stung.
Unmoved he answered: "Queen, I strive to do
My duty only, like the sages true;
Nor would I, with a soul athirst for gain,
False to my promise, in the world remain.
All I can do to please my father, think
Already done: from death I would not shrink
One duty, paramount of duties still,
Is that a son should do his father's will.
By him unbidden, if the word thou give,
Will I an exile in the forest live.

Couldst thou no virtue in my nature see
That thou must crave of him, not ask of me?
This day I go in Dandak's wilds to dwell:
First to my mother I must bid farewell,
And comfort Sita. Thine the charge must rest
That Bharat listen to his sire's behest,
And keep the kingdom happy and secure:
This is the law that ever shall endure."

In speechless woe the hapless father heard,
And wept with bitter cry, but spoke no word.
Then bowing at the senseless monarch's feet,
And stern Kaikeyi's, for such love unmeet,
Once round the pair his circling steps he bent,
Then from the bower the glorious exile went.
Him followed Lakshman, sweet Sumitra's child,
With angry weeping eyes so sad and wild.
And Rama saw, nor turned his eyes away,
The sacred vessels ranged for that great day;
And golden chalices, whose waters poured
Upon his head would have ordained him lord.
He saw, and round them in due honour paced,
His eye no anguish showed, his foot no haste.
Still on his brow, with lofty hope o'erthrown,
Shone the great glory which was all his own;
So doth the moon, through the world's love, retain
Delicious splendour in the days of wane.

MOTHER AND SON.

Rama gees from the presence of his afflicted father and exulting step-mother to pay a farewell visit to Kausalya, who is full of joyful anticipations on her son's account.

On to his mother's splendid bower he went,
And found the queen on holy rites intent.
There oil, and rice, and brimming vases stood,
With wreaths of flowers, and curds, and cates, and wood.
She with her thin cheek pale with many a fast,
And many a night in painful vigil past,
In linen robes of purest white arrayed,
To Lakshmi, Queen of Heaven, her offerings made.
Soon as she saw the darling of her soul,
As a fond mare who springs to meet her foal,
To greet her son, unseen so long, she flew,
And round his neck her tender arms she threw:
" May all the glories of thy royal line,"
She cried, with kisses on his brow, " be thine.
Be wise and mighty like thy sires of old,
Be good and noble, pious, lofty souled.
This day thy father's faithful love is shown:
This day he sets thee on his ancient throne."

Then answered Rama, " Dearest lady, know
That danger threatens, fraught with mighty woe.
My father's choice this day makes Bharat heir;
And I must hence to Dandak's wood, and there

Living on fruit and honey, hermit's food,
Pass twice seven dreary years in solitude."

Swift as a Sal branch, by the woodman lopt
In some primeval grove, the lady dropt
And lay upon the ground. So falls a mare
Beneath the load she strives in vain to bear.
And Rama raised her up, and brusht away
The dust that on her arms and shoulders lay.
"A grief more sore" she cried, "I ne'er could mourn
If thou had never, O my son, been born;
Yet, well I know, their childless fate, to those
Who pine for offspring, is the crown of woes.
I, eldest queen, to those I scorn, must bend,
And let my rival's taunt my bosom rend.
What woman's lot can be so hard as mine,
In endless woe and mourning doomed to pine?
Have they not scorned me when my son was near?
And death will follow when thou art not here.
'Twas ne'er my lot my husband's love to gain,
And now I'm mockt by proud Kaikeyi's train;
And those who served me once, a faithless band,
Now far aloof in gloomy silence stand.
How shall I brook her scolding tongue to hear,
And, better far than she, her anger fear?
Since thou wast born ('tis seventeen years ago),
I've lookt to thee one day to end my woe.
Now what remains but shame and grief, a share
Of trouble heavier than my soul can bear!
How will my gloomy days go darkly by
Without thy moon-bright face to cheer mine eye?

Alas! my cares thy tender years to train,
And all my vows and fasts and prayers were vain!
Hard is my heart, or surely it had burst
When the wild rush of sorrow reacht it first;
As in the Rains no river bank can hold
The headlong torrent from the mountains rolled.
Ah no! my death is not allowed by fate,
Nor opes for me the Gloomy King his gate:
He will not take me to his home away,
A lion pitying his weeping prey.
Death will not listen to a wretch's cry,
Nor take his soul ere fate would have him die,
Or I, bereaved of my son, had fled
To Yama's[1] home, and been among the dead.
Why should I live without thee? I will go
After thee, Rama, though my steps be slow,
As a poor cow, in her great love, will run
Watching the wanderings of her little one."

While sad Kausalya wept and groaned and sighed,
Thus, moved with righteous anger, Lakshman cried:
"O venerable queen, I like it not
That Rama, victim of a woman's plot,
Should fly an exile to the woods, and leave
The land to languish and his friends to grieve.
The king, luxurious, doting, old, and weak,
Will hear her voice and, as she orders, speak.
But why should Rama, pure of sin and stain,
Flee from his kingdom to a life of pain?

[1] The Indian Pluto.

What man could ever, deaf to duty's call,
Forsake his godlike son beloved of all?
What son, that father's senseless will, obey,
In second childhood 'neath a woman's sway?
Come, Rama, come, and, ere this plot be known,
Accept my succour and secure the throne.
Before thy face what foe will dare to stand
When thou art guarded by my good right hand?
Nay, like the grisly Monarch of the Dead,
Thine eye alone will strike the bold with dread.
Or if, thou wilt, mine arrows and my bow
Shall lay all dwellers in Ayodhya low:
So shall the foemen find mine arm is strong;
The patient ever are the prey of wrong.
Nay, were it not that queen Kaikeyi's art
Has swayed our father and destroyed his heart,
My voice should now his ruthless hate arraign,
And cry, The monarch shall be slain, be slain.
Queen, by this bow and by my faith I swear,
To thy dear Rama such the love I bear,
Come life come death, our path shall be the same
To the wild forest or the deadly flame.
Come, try my love, and let me prove my might
Before thy presence and in Rama's sight:
Before my power thy woe shall flee away,
As the night flees before the morning ray."

"O Rama, hear him," thus with streaming eyes,
Cried sad Kausalya, "for his words are wise.
Wilt thou, obedient to my rival's will,
Please her who hates thee, and thy mother kill?

If love and honour to thy sire be due,
Hast thou no honour for thy mother too?
My life were woe without thee, but how sweet,
With thee, dear son, though grass were all my meat!
But if no prayers thy firm resolve can bend,
I fly to death, my hopeless woe to end;
And thou, thy mother's murderer, wilt bear
The punishment of Hell and torment there."

"Forgive me, mother," thus the hero spake.
"I have no power my sire's command to break.
See, at thy honoured feet I bend me low:
Once more forgive me, for I needs must go.
Not I the first this path of duty tread,
Of yore 'twas trodden by the mighty dead.
Now let me hear, dear queen, thy kind farewell;
But if I go in distant wilds to dwell,
'Tis not for ever, mother, that I leave
My home and thee. Again thou shalt receive
Thy son with rapture, all his exile o'er;
Then be thou comforted and grieve no more."
"If thou wilt listen to no prayers of mine,
Go forth," she cried, "thou best of Raghu's line!
Go forth, my darling, and return with speed,
And tread the path where noble spirits lead.
May Virtue ever on thy steps attend,
And thee, her lover, from all woe defend.
May all the Gods to whom thy vows are paid,
And all the mighty saints afford their aid.

The heavenly arms, that Viswamitra[1] gave,
Thy precious life in hours of danger save!
Thy filial love and meek obedience arm
Thy soul, my Rama, like a mystic charm!
May every shrine where sacred grass is spread,
And every altar where the flame is fed,
Lake and wild mountain, bush and towering tree,
Give ready succour, O my son, to thee.
May Vishnu, Brahma, and the Sun befriend,
And all the powers their high protection lend.
The years, the seasons, months, and nights and days,
And hours, watch over thee in all thy ways!
Eternal Scripture and the Law revealed
To ancient sages be thy trusty shield!
The War-God aid thee, and the Moon on high,
And wise Brihaspati be ever nigh.
Thy help be Narad[2] and the sainted Seven,
And the great limitary lords of heaven![3]
Yea, these shall guard thee, when their praise I sing,
The hills, the waters, and the waters' king.
The sky and ether, earth and wandering air,
Protect thee ever with their fostering care!
Each lunar mansion be for thee benign:
With happier light for thee the planets shine!
Thou shalt not fear, by guardian angels screened,
The savage giant or night-roving fiend.

1 A saint, the friend and preceptor of Rama.

2 A son of Brahma.

3 Eight Gods, Regents of the four quarters and intermediate points of the compass.

Before thy steps let cruel tigers flee,
Let bears and lions never injure thee,
And mighty elephants that wander wild
Forbear to touch thy life, my noble child.
May all thy ways be happy! may success
With golden fruit thy hope and labour bless!
Loved by all Gods around, above, below,
Go forth, my son, my pride and glory, go!"

Then on his knees before her Rama fell,
Prest her dear feet and said his last farewell;
And, radiant with the light her blessings lent,
To Sita's home his anxious steps he bent.

THE TRIUMPH OF LOVE.

But Rama's hardest trial yet remains, the parting from Sita, his lovely and beloved wife. He briefly tells her of his altered lot, and bids her in his absence carefully discharge her duties to the Gods, his father, the three queens, the new King Bharat and his brothers. She tells him that man and wife are not thus to be parted, and declares that whithersoever he goes she will go also. In vain he sets before her the dangers and miseries that wait on banishment. Truth smiles at fear; and Love sees a Paradise in the wild with him. Rama yields to the passionate prayers of his devoted wife, and allows her to accompany him to the forest.[1]

As through his stately halls the hero past,
His eye was drooping and his brow o'ercast.
And Sita rose and trembled, quick to trace
The thought and sorrow on his darkened face;
For his strong bosom could no longer bear
The load of anguish that was heavy there.
Soon as she markt the clammy drops that hung
On his pale cheek, she cried, with faltering tongue:
"What ails thee, O my lord? This happy day
Should see thee joyful: all but thou are gay.
Why does no royal canopy, like foam
For its white beauty, shade thee to thy home?

[1] A version of part of this scene, from Gorresio's edition of the Bengal recension of the Ramayana, has appeared, under the title of "Sita," in *Idylls from the Sanskrit*. The main features are the same in both, but the details slightly differ.

Where are the tuneful bards, thy deeds to sing?
Where are the fans that wave before the king?
Why doth the city send no merry throng
To bring thee home with melody and song?
Why doth no gilded car thy triumph lead,
With four brave horses of the swiftest breed?
No favoured elephant precede the crowd,
Like a black mountain or a thunder-cloud?
No herald march in front of thee to hold
The precious burthen of thy throne of gold?
If thou be king, ordained this day, then why
This sorry plight, pale cheek, and gloomy eye?"

Thus Sita questioned in her wild suspense.
And Rama said: "My father sends me hence
An exile to the forest: hear me tell
The story, Sita, as it all befell.
Of old, to queen Kaikeyi, bound by oath,
Two boons he granted: now she claims them both.
All was prepared for me: my father now
Is forced by Duty's mightier law to bow;
So Bharat sits upon the throne, and I
For twice seven years to distant forests fly.
Only to see thee ere we part, I came.
And now, dear Sita, never praise my name
In Bharat's presence: others' praise to hear
Is never welcome to a monarch's ear.
To him my father gives divided sway:
Do thou with willing love his rule obey.
With tender care the king's desire prevent
Be ever gentle, humble, and content.

I go : be firm and strong, my noble spouse,
Keep well thy fasts and guard thy holy vows.
Rise from thy bed when day begins to break,
And to the Gods thy constant offerings make.
Then let the king thy duteous thoughts engage,
And cheer Kausalya worn with woe and age.
Then to the consort-queens thy love be shown :
They are my mothers even as mine own.
And O, forget not, Rama's brothers claim,
Loved like his life, the love of Rama's dame.
And never vex king Bharat's soul, for he
Is lord of all the land, our house, and thee.
Then here, obedient to his will, remain :
Honour thy king and all thy vows maintain."

"Beseems," she cried, "this speech thy royal race,
To thee a blot, to me a foul disgrace ?
Master of weapons, lord of deadly strife,
Hear thou the duty of a warrior's wife.
Know that the father, mother, brother, son,
Obtain the lot their former deeds have won.
The wife alone her husband's fate must share,
And in thy trouble I my part will bear.
For not on father, mother, son, or friend,
But on her husband, must the wife depend.
And, if thou seek the wood, thy wife has sworn
To smooth thy path, nor let thy feet be torn.
No guile is in me : from thy bosom throw
The dregs of doubt, and give me leave to go.
I spurn the terrace and the pleasant seat
Mine be the joy to guard thy cherisht feet.

Obedient ever to my parents' sway,
I will not hearken if they bid me stay.
I will go forth, the lonely wood to roam,
The lion's dwelling and the tiger's home,
Happy and heedless, from all terror free,
Careless of empire, caring but for thee.
With thee, delighted, will I wander where
Blooms, dropping honey, scent the woodland air.
Obeying thee and keeping still my vow
I will not tremble by thy side, for thou
Wouldst keep a stranger safe, and, sure, thine arm
Will guard thy Sita from all fear of harm.
I will not be a charge to thee : sweet fruits
The trees will yield me, and the earth her roots.
I will go first and, treading down the grass,
Make the way pleasant for my love to pass ;
On the soft turf disclose my gathered store,
And sit and banquet when thy meal is o'er.
O, how I long, dear lord, to gaze my fill,
Guarded by thee, on lake, and wood, and hill ;
See the red lilies in their native springs,
And gay flamingoes with their rosy wings !
And o'er my limbs those pleasant waters poured
Shall banish languor, O my large-eyed lord.
A thousand years would seem a single day
If spent with thee, but, were my love away,
Heaven would not charm me : O, be sure of this,
Without my love there is no heaven, no bliss."

Lost in deep thought awhile the hero stood,
And feared to lead her to the lonely wood.

With soothing words he strove her tears to dry,
And gently answered with a moistened eye :
" O virtuous daughter of a noble line,
To hear my words thy tender heart incline
Here, duteous ever, still in peace remain :
Life in the woods is naught but grief and pain.
There roars the lion in his rocky cave,
Loud as the torrents down the hill that rave
There savage beasts in horrid ambush lie
And rend the heedless wretch who passes by.
Floods, where the crocodile delights to play,
And furious elephants, the eye dismay.
Then on the gale the wolf's long howl is borne
Through a wide wilderness of sand and thorn.
On the cold ground or on a scanty heap
Of gathered leaves the homeless wretch must sleep,
And stay his hunger with what fruit the blast
Hurls from the branches for his sad repast.
A coat of bark or skin his only wear,
Rough and untrimmed must be his matted hair.
Now on a snake the heedless foot will fall,
Now in thy path a deadly scorpion crawl,
And slimy reptiles creeping from the lake,
And clouds of gnats, thy troubled slumber break.
Enough, dear love; the wood is full of fear:
Remain, my Sita, and be happy here."

Then Sita spoke once more with weeping eyes,
Her voice half mastered by her sobs and sighs:
" The woe, the terror, all the toil and pain,
Joined with thy love, to me are joy and gain.

Lion and tiger, elephant and boar,
And all the monsters thou hast counted o'er,
Soon as my Rama's glorious form they see,
In trembling fear will turn away and flee.
Not Indra's self, the ruler of the sky,
Would dare to harm me when my lord is nigh.
Long years ago I heard a sage foretell
That in the woods should be my fate to dwell:
The time is come; now make that promise true,
And when thou goest take thy Sita too.
O, let me go; whate'er I may endure,
Following thee, will make my soul more pure;
So joy shall crown me in the after life,
For thou art God unto thy loving wife.
Hear the high truth which saintly priests declare:
The after life rejoins the wedded pair.
But if thou wilt to no entreaties bend,
Poison or flood or flame my life shall end.
Fear not for me; when by thy side I go
My happy feet will never weary grow.
Though wild and rough the thorny ways I tread,
They shall feel softer than a silken bed.
When the wild wind with dust my raiment dims,
I'll call it perfume to refresh my limbs.
And when with thee in grassy glades I lie,
Watching the landscape with delighted eye,
Till, by thy side, I gently sink to rest,
What thing on earth shall be so richly blest?
The fruit thy dear hand gives me there to eat,
Little or much, shall be, like *Amrit*, sweet.

Ne'er will I murmur at my lot, or grieve
For mother, father, or the home I leave.
My food shall be wild fruit, the flower, the weed:
I will not vex thee by a word or deed.
With thee is heaven, where'er thou art not, hell:
O, lead me hence that I in heaven may dwell."
Then with a bitter cry her arms she flung
Round Rama's neck, and there in anguish clung:
While from her eyes pure floods, as from a pair
Of lotuses, poured down at every prayer.

He gently held her, raised her drooping head,
And staid the sweet soul that had wellnigh fled:
"Not heaven shall bribe me from my wife to part.
I knew not, love, the strength of thy fond heart;
And hence in doubt thy prayer I first denied,
Though naught can harm thee by thy Rama's side.
Yea, thou wast formed by Heaven to share my fate,
To soothe my sorrows and divide their weight.
As powerless I to leave my love behind,
As a high saint his pity for mankind.
And now my duty leads me far away:
My sire commands it and I must obey.
Whate'er the order that my parents give,
I yield obedience, or must cease to live.
No, Sita, not the sacrificial blaze,
True heart, or liberal hand, or lip of praise,
Will with such lasting joy the spirit fill
As glad obedience to a father's will.
Come to the wood and aid my duties there,
But first at home thy helping hand prepare.

Arise, dear wife, nor let thy steps be slow,
Scatter our treasures quickly ere we go.
Bring forth thy corn and oil the poor to feast,
Give gold and jewels to each white-robed priest;
Gems and rich raiment, all thou hast beside,
Among thy maidens and the men divide."

Then Lakshman's eyes with generous tears o'erflowed,
As his breast laboured with its grievous load.
He with fond touch his brother's feet carest,
And thus the hero and his wife addrest:
" Is such the purpose of thy changeless mind?
I with my trusty bow will walk behind.
Thy distant way through forest wilds will lead,
Where many a bird and gallant stag may bleed.
I would not leave thee to arise a God,
Though heaven and earth and hell obeyed my nod."

" Dear as my life, my good and faithful friend,
Mine own dear brother," Rama cried, " attend.
Then were Sumitra of her hope bereft,
And sad Kausalya with no guardian left.
He who rains gifts, as Indra rains above,
Lies a poor captive in the snares of love;
And she, proud captor, now a queen indeed,
Will reck but little of her rival's need.
Thine be the sacred duty to protect
Our honoured mothers from the queen's neglect."

" O Rama, fear not." Lakshman thus replied;
" In Bharat's love and Bharat's care confide.
If through his crime the kingdom suffer ill,
My vengeful hand the traitor's blood shall spill.

Yea, though auxiliar worlds were ranged in aid,
They should not save him; be not thou afraid;
For queen Kausalya, from her ample stores,
Can raise a host like me to guard her doors:
Her thousand hamlets, rich with golden grain,
Will keep her nobly and a regal train.
Turn me not back: allow the earnest claim
Which all will own and hardly thou canst blame.
I shall rejoice, and thou wilt fain confess
Thy brother's presence makes thy labour less.
For in my hand I'll bear my shafts and bow,
A spade and basket o'er my shoulder throw.
I'll go before thee, and with watchful care
The way for Sita and for thee prepare.
I'll fetch thee roots and berries, ripe and sweet,
And the best fruits that gentle hermits eat.
Thou shalt with Sita on the slopes recline,
And all the labour shall be only mine."

And Rama answered, joying at his speech:
"Then seek thy friends and bid farewell to each;
And those two bows of heavenly fabric bring
Which ocean's lord erst gave Videha's king; [1]
Those death-fraught quivers, coats of steel-proof mail,
And swords whose flashes make the sunbeams pale."

[1] Janaka, father of Sita.

FAREWELL!

Rama, his wife, and brother walk through the streets, crowded with mourning citizens, to the palace of Dasaratha. They bid the king farewell, and then leave Ayodhya amid the tears and lamentations of the people.

Their gold and gems among the Brahmans shared,
The bows were brought, the swords and mail prepared,
On which fair Sita with her faultless hand,
Set here a flower, there tied a silken band.
Then to the palace walked the royal three,
For the last time the aged king to see,
Through crowds that filled, as for a festive show,
Street, balcony, and roof, and portico.

"Ah! look, our hero, ever wont to ride,
Leading an army in its pomp and pride,—
Now only Lakshman, faithful to the end,
And his true wife, his weary steps attend.
Though his bright soul has known the sweets of power,
Though his free hand poured gifts in endless shower,
Yet firm in duty, resolute and brave,
He keeps the promise that his father gave.
And she, whose sweet face, delicately fair,
Not e'en the wandering spirits of the air
Might look upon, unveiling to the day
Walks, seen of all, along the open way.
Alas, her beauty! Ah, that tender form!
How will it change beneath the sun and storm!

How will the piercing cold, the rain, the heat,
Pale her dear lips and stain her perfect feet!
Come, all ye, mourners, share his weal and woe,
And follow Rama wheresoe'er he go.
Let us arise, our wives and children call,
And leave our fields and gardens, homes and all.
Our houses, empty of their store of grain,
With grass-grown courtyard and deserted lane:
Our ruined chambers, where the voice is still
Of women singing as they turn the mill:
Groves, where no children sport in thoughtless glee,
Nor elders sit beneath the mango-tree:
The falling shop, with none to buy or sell,
The pond choked up with weeds, the broken well:
Neglected temples, whence the Gods have fled,
O'errun with rats, with dust and dirt o'erspread;
Where floats no incense on the evening air,
No hum of worship, and no Brahman's prayer:
Where broken vessels strew the unswept floor,
And the chain rusts upon the mouldering door—
These let the greedy queen, Kaikeyi gain,
And triumph in her melancholy reign.
Our town shall be a w lderness: where he,
Our Rama, lives, the wood our town shall be.
The snake shall leave his hole, the bear his den,
And settle in the empty homes of men."
Such were the words of sorrow that the throng
Spoke loudly out as Rama past along,
And his hard fate in faithful love bewailed;
Yet not for this his lofty spirit failed.

On to the place of the king he prest,
And thus Sumantra at the gate addrest:
"I pray thee, haste and let my father know
That Rama craves a blessing ere he go."
He lingered not, but hastened where the king,
Lord of the world, lay sadly sorrowing;
Changed, like the sun behind a misty cloud;
Like the quencht flame which dust and ashes shroud;
Like a broad lake with its sweet waters dried.
With a slow faltering voice Sumantra cried:
"Long be thy days, O king! Thy Rama waits,
Thy lion-lord of men, before the gates.
His weeping friends his last farewell have heard,
Graced with a precious gift and pleasant word;
And now he longs his father's face to see,
And take a blessing, ere he go, of thee."

"Haste," cried the king, "my queens and ladies call,
And bid my servants throng into the hall."
Quick at the monarch's word he called each dame,
And half seven hundred at the summons came.
When all were present, at the king's behest,
Rama and Lakshman in their armour drest,
Come toward the hall, with anxious ladies lined,
And gentle Sita meekly came behind.
But the old king, ere Rama yet was nigh,
Sprang from his throne, and with a bitter cry
Ran forth to meet him: but his limbs gave way,
And falling prostrate on the ground he lay.
And Rama threw him by his father's side,
And gently called him, but no voice replied.

Then with a mighty wail the hall was rent:
A thousand women, in one wild lament,
Cried, Rama, Rama! 'mid the silver sound
Of tinkling ornaments their wrists that bound.
The king, unconscious, on a couch was laid,
And weeping Sita lent her tender aid,
And with her healing care restored him: then
Rama spoke, reverent, to the king of men:

"O father, thou both sire and sovereign art:
Bless me, I pray thee, for to-day we part.
Lakshman and Sita will not here remain:
Counsel is useless and entreaty vain.
Refuse them not, but grant thy kind consent
That they may follow as their heart is bent.
And now as kings dismiss their people, so,
Grieve not, O lord, but bless and let us go."
He stood expecting when the king should speak;
Who answered: "Rama, I am old and weak,
By Queen Kaikeyi's cruel guile misled:
Rule thou Ayodhya in thy father's stead."
And Rama cried: "A thousand years retain
Thy sceptre, King: I have no wish to reign.
I in the wild my destined years will spend,
And clasp thy feet returning when they end.
This populous land, which I this day resign,
Let Bharat rule, with all its corn and kine.
And from Kaikeyi do not thou withhold
Aught thy tongue promised in the days of old.
By thy good deeds and by thy truth I swear,
I crave not heaven or all the glories there:

Wealth, lordship, life are worthless in mine eyes ;
One thing alone above the rest I prize,
That thou, my king and sire, shouldst still remain
Untoucht in honour, without spot or stain.
Weep not for me : thy troubled bosom still,
Nor hope, with tears, to change my changeless will.
My word is pledged as well as thine, for know
Kaikeyi prayed me, and I sware to go.
Grieve not : the forest will have charms for me,
Where sweet birds sing and wild deer wander free.
Swift will the years of easy exile run,
And thou once more shalt see restored thy son."

" Make ready," cried the king, "a mighty force,
With cars and elephants and foot and horse :
Equip them nobly with the utmost care ;
Silver and gold and priceless gems prepare.
Let various traders, with the wealth they sell,
Come from the city, and the concourse swell ;
And singing-women, fair of form and face,
The royal progress of prince Rama grace.
Let every noble whom he counts his friend,
Enricht with precious gifts, his lord attend.
Let the best arms in many a ponderous wain,
And skilful huntsmen, follow in his train.
It may be that the banisht prince may blunt
Each sting of memory in the eager hunt,
And, as he sucks the wild-bee's balmy spoil,
Forget his kingdom and enjoy the toil.
Let all my gold, and boundless wealth of corn,
To the wild forest, where he goes, be borne.

For it will sweeten the poor exile's lot
To sacrifice in every holy spot:
To give rich offerings as he roams, and meet
Each saintly hermit in his lone retreat."

And Rama answered: "Useless, Sire, to me
The host, the riches, and the pomp would be:
For I, the world and all its lusts resigned,
Have left its pride and joys and cares behind.
My home is now the wilderness, and there
The hermit's life awaits, the hermit's fare.
Give me no banners o'er my head to float,
All I now covet is the hermit's coat."

And queen Kaikeyi, with unblushing brow,
Cried, " See, 'tis ready: take and wear it now."
The hero took it from her hand, and threw
His own fine robe upon the ground, and drew
The rough bark mantle on. So Lakshman braced,
His dress removed, the bark around his waist.
But modest Sita in her silks arrayed,
Eyed the strange mantle trembling and afraid:
As from Kaikeyi's hand the coat she took,
She viewed it with a startled wondering look,
As, in the brake beside the stream, a deer
Looks at the hunter's snare with doubt and fear.
With weeping eyes, like a poor bleating lamb
That runs with trembling feet to find its dam,
She nestled closely to her Rama's side,
And in her soft low faltering accents, cried:
" Tell me how hermits, dwelling in the wood,
Tie their bark mantles on." Perplext she stood,

Shrinking in modest dread, while one small hand
Strove at the neck to join the rugged band.

Then, quickly hastening, Ráma, first and best
Of Virtue's children, o'er her silken vest
Fastened the coat of bark. Then rose a cry
From all the women, and each tender eye
Drop water: "Rama, leave us Sita; she
Shares not the cruel doom that falls on thee.
Hear us, we pray thee; let thy Sita stay,
To bless our sight while thou art far away."

Then spoke the sovereign's venerable guide,
Sainted Vasishtha, as he deeply sighed
Looking on Sita in her coat of bark:
"O cruel queen Kaikeyi, fell and dark
In purpose, evil-hearted; thou disgrace
To thy great father and thy royal race:
Deceiver of thy lord, thy plots are vain;
For still will Sita in her home remain,
And sit as rightful ruler on the throne
Prepared for Rama, till he claim his own.
The pair who live in wedlock's sweet control
Form but one heart and mind and self and soul:
She, Rama's self, shall Rama's kingdom sway,
And we with joy her gentle rule obey.
If she resolve to share her husband's woes,
We all will follow where our lady goes.
Our wives and children, our young men and maids,
Will roam with Rama through the forest glades:
Nay, thy son Bharat, and Satrughna, too,
Will to Ayodhya bid a long adieu,

Around their limbs the hermit's garb to fold,
And serve their elder brother, as of old.
Do thou, rejoicing in the people's bane,
Enjoy, 'mid empty homes, thy lonely reign:
For 'tis no kingdom where our king is not;
He makes an empire in the wildest spot."

Sumantra, bowing with his reverent head,
Upraised his suppliant hands, to Rama said:
"My ready car, O royal prince, ascend,
And where thou wilt, my rapid course I bend."
With cheerful heart, her toilet task complete,
The Rose of women rose[1] and took her seat.
And Rama next and Lakshman true and bold,
Sprang on the sun-bright chariot deckt with gold.
Sumantra, mounted, urged each willing steed,
Of noble lineage, like the wind for speed.

Then rose to heaven one universal shriek;
And the whole city, old, young, strong, and weak,
Rusht toward the car, as, from the scorching sun,
The panting herds to shaded water run.
Before the chariot and behind they hung,
And cried, with weeping eyes, as there they clung:
"O check thy steeds; drive slower, we implore:
And let us see our Rama's face once more.
His mother's heart is, surely, barred with steel,
Or it had broken with the pangs we feel.
Sita, well done! Videha's flower and pride,
Still, like his shadow, by thy husband's side:

[1] *Âruroha varároha.*

Cheering his path with thy loved presence still,
As the sun never sets on Meru's hill.[1]
And thou, O Lakshman, shalt have honour too,
Serving thy brother with a love so true:
Yea, noblest honour for thy noble deeds,
For this the path to heaven and bliss that leads."

Thus in their sorrow cried the weeping throng:
"Drive on," said Rama, "we delay too long."
Perplext, the driver could not both obey;
"Hasten," cried Rama: cried the people, "Stay."
From the men's eyes the tears in torrents flowed,
And laid the dust upon the royal road;
While, in the woe that rent their bosoms, all
The women rained their tears, like drops that fall
From the drencht lotus-leaves upon the lake,
Which darting fish, glittering under, shake.
The king, as Rama from his sight was borne,
Fell, like a Sall tree by the roots uptorn;
And the loud wailing cry that rent the skies
Made Rama for a moment turn his eyes
Where his sad mother and her train stood round
His hapless father fainting on the ground.
Then, as a young thing, in the meshes caught,
Looks to its mother with a quick glance fraught

[1] A sacred mountain placed by the Hindus in the centre of the seven continents of which the earth is made up. It is said to be 84,000 *yojanas* high (*a yojana* is reckoned variously at four and nine miles). Its summit is a residence of the God Brahma.

With utter anguish, bound by duty's chain,
Gazing in most intolerable pain,
One long last look of love and grief he cast,
Then urged the steeds till out of sight he past.

THE HERMIT'S SON.

"But the exiles were no sooner gone than the aged monarch drooped in sadness. 'Six days he sat and mourned, and pined for Rama all that weary time.' In the middle of the seventh night a crime, inadvertently committed in his youth, rose up in his mind: he sought sympathy from Kausalya, his first wife, the mother of the banished Rama, and asked her to listen to his tale, for to this he attributed his present affliction."—MRS. SPEIR.

Heavy was his soul within him, still in Dasaratha's breast
Memory of woe kept brooding and forbade the king to rest.
Deep despair upon his spirit, mourning for his Rama, lay,
As when clouds have veiled the glory of the parting Lord of Day,
As he thought with bitter anguish of the deed his hand had done,
Spake he sorrowing to Kausalya sighing weeping for her son:
"Art thou waking, mournful lady? Give me all thy listening ear;
Hearken to a tale of sorrow, to an ancient deed of fear.
Surely each shall reap the harvest of his actions here below:
Righteous deed shall bear a blessing, sin shall ever bring forth woe.
'Tis a deed of youthful folly brings on me this evil day,
As a young child tasting poison eats his death in heedless play.

Twas a day of early rain-time, filling my young soul with love,
When the sun had dried the earth-dews with his hot beams from above,
And in highest heaven turning journeyed on his southward road,
Speeding to the gloomy region, the Departed's sad abode.
Balmy cool the air was breathing, welcome clouds were floating by,
Humming bees, with joyful music swelled the glad wild peacock's cry.
Their wing-feathers wet with bathing, birds, slow flying to the trees,
Rested in the topmost branches waving to the western breeze.
Like the Ocean many-twinkling, gold-shot with gay peacock's sheen,
Gleaming with the fallen rain-drops, sea-bright all the hills were seen;
While like serpents, winding swiftly, torrents from the mountain's side
Hissed along, some brightly flashing, turbid some and ochre-dyed,
With my bow in that glad season to fair Sarju's stream I drove,
Bent to try my archer prowess in a dark and stately grove.
There I lay in ambush hidden by the river's reedy side,
Where the beasts that roam the forest sought at eve the cooling tide.
Hark! a sound of troubled water from the neighbouring stream I heard:
All was dark and still around me, not a breath the branches stirred.

Eager to lay low the monster forth a glittering shaft I drew;
Poisonous as serpent's venom from my string the arrow flew.
Then I heard a bitter wailing and a voice of direst pain
Calling out, 'Ah me, unhappy! Dearest father, I am slain!'
Writhing on the bank in anguish sobbingly one cried, 'Ah me!
Wherefore has this arrow smitten a poor harmless devotee?
Here at eve to fill my pitcher to this lonely stream I came:
Tell me whom I have offended, who my harmless act can blame.
Who could have the heart to kill me, me the guiltless hermit's child,
Drinking from the stream and eating fruit and herbs he gathers wild?
Would the slayer strip my body? He will find but scanty spoil:
Coat of bark and deerskin mantle hardly will repay his toil.
'Tis not for myself I sorrow: from mine aged parents torn,
Long their stay and only succour, 'tis for their sad fate I mourn.
Who will feed them when I perish? wretched man, whoe'er thou art,
Thou hast murdered father, mother, offspring, all with one fell dart.'
Horror seized my soul within me, and my mind was well-nigh fled,
In the stilly calm of evening as I heard the words he said.
Rushing forward through the bushes on the river-bank I spied
Lying low a young ascetic with my shaft deep in his side.
With his matted hair dishevelled, and his pitcher cast away,
From his side the life blood ebbing, smeared with dust and gore he lay.

Then he fixt his eyes upon me: scarcely could my spirit brook,
As these bitter words he uttered, that long last departing look:
'Only to fetch water came I: tell me, wherefore do I bleed?
Have I sinned against thee, monarch? Done thee wrong in word or deed?
Ah! I'm not thine only victim: cruel king, thy heedless dart
Pierces too a father's bosom and an aged mother's heart.
They, my parents, blind and feeble, from this hand alone can drink:
When I come not, thirsting, hoping, sadly down in death they'll sink.
Naught from lore of studied Scripture, naught from penance do I gain,
For my hapless father knows not his dear son is lying slain.
Ah! and if he knew me dying powerless to save were he,
As a tree can never rescue from the axe a fated tree.
Hasten to him, son of Raghu. Tell my father of my fate,
Lest his wrath like fire consume thee. Hasten, ere it be too late.
There within the shady forest is my father's hermitage:
Go, entreat him, son of Raghu, lest he curse thee in his rage.'
Thus he spake, and I down-kneeling, drew the arrow from his side:
Then the hermit, rich in penance, fixt his eyes on me and died.
Motionless I stood in sorrow: pondering in anxious thought
How to minister most kindly to the woe my hand had wrought.
From the stream I filled the pitcher, and, fast speeding through the wood,
Reached the middle of the forest where the lowly cottage stood.

Talking of their son's long absence, a poor aged sightless pair,
Like two birds with clipt wings, helpless, none to guide them, sat they there.
Sadly, slowly I approached them, by my rash deed left forlorn;
Crusht with terror was my spirit, and my heart with anguish torn.
At the sound of coming footsteps thus I heard the old man say:
'Dear son, bring the water quickly: thou hast been too long away,
Bathing in the stream, or playing, heedless how the minutes past:
Come, thy mother longeth for thee. Come, and cheer her heart at last.
Be not angry, mine own darling. Thou hast never vext us yet,
And if I have spoken harshly do forgive me and forget.
Thou art thy poor parents' succour, eyes art thou unto the blind:
Speak, on thee our lives are resting. Why so silent and unkind?'
Thus I heard, yet deeper grieving, and in fresh augmented woe,
Spake to the bereaved father with words faltering and slow:
'I am not thy son, O hermit, but the ruler of the land,
Plunged with thee in woe and mourning by my own accursed hand.
There on Sarju's bank I wandered with my arrows and my bow
Bent to lay some prowling lion or a thirsty tiger low.
Then I heard a sound of drinking: all the place around was dark,
But I sent the deadly arrow, ah! too truly to the mark.
Bounding swiftly from my ambush to the river's bank I hied,
Where a hermit's son lay dying with my arrow in his side.

Forth I drew the deadly weapon. Then his last lament was given
To his aged helpless parents, and his spirit went to heaven.
Thus thy son, O saintly hermit, through my haste and folly fell;
Let deep sorrow win thy pardon for the deed I scarce can tell.'
As he heard my mournful story, pouring down his aged cheek
Came the torrent of his sorrow, and his voice came low and weak:
'King, hadst thou concealed this horror, this blood-shedding left untold,
On thy head the sin had fallen with its fruit ten thousandfold.
For a Warrior stained with murder, of a hermit above all,
From his high estate, blood-guilty, were he Indra's self, must fall.
Lead us, king, by thee bereaved: lead us to the fatal place:
Let us fold our darling's body in a last and long embrace.'
By the hand I led the mourners to the river where he lay:
Fondly claspt the sightless parents in their arms the death-cold clay.
Bowed down by their load of sorrow sank they by the dead boy's side,
And the sage in lamentation lifted up his voice and cried:
'Hast thou not a greeting for me? Am not I thy father, dear?
Answer but one word, my darling. Wherefore art thou lying here?
Art thou angry with thy father? Speak to me, beloved one!
Surely thou wast ever duteous; look then on thy mother, son.
Come dear child, embrace thy father, put thy little hand in mine:
Let me hear thee sweetly prattle some fond playful word of thine.

Who will read me now the Scripture, filling my old heart with joy?
Who, when evening rites are ended, cheer me mourning for my boy?
Who will tend the helpless parents, fetch us water from the spring?
Who will guide our feeble footsteps? Who will fruits and berries bring?
Can I feed thine aged mother till her weary life is o'er?
Can I soothe her ever longing for the son who comes no more?
Stay, dear child, nor fly so quickly to grim Yama's dark abode:
Stay, thy father and thy mother will go with thee on the road.
In the wild wood all deserted, none to aid us in our need,
Quickly will thine aged parents tread the path for all decreed.
Guiltless boy by sinner murdered, join thine own immortal band
In the heaven of slaughtered heroes slain on earth by other's hand.
Hasten to thy blissful mansion; welcome shalt thou be to those
Who fell nobly here in battle with their bold front to their foes.'
Then the funeral rites were finisht by the parents' loving care,
And again the sage addrest me as I stood a suppliant there:
'Thou hast slain my well-beloved, killed mine only child, O king:
Kill me too, the childless father: death no longer has a sting.
But thou shalt not go unpunisht. Wretched youth, thy breast shall know
Somewhat of the pangs I suffer, a bereaved father's woe.
Thus I lay my curse upon thee;—for this slaughter done to-day,
Thou for a dear son shalt sorrow, and thy life the debt shall pay.'

THE TRIAL OF TRUTH.

After Dasarath's death Bharata refused to accept the insignia of royalty, which according to Hindu law was the heritage of his elder brother. We are not told how his mother behaved when he thus refused to aid her wicked schemes for his advancement; but the Council resolved, that if he would not be King himself, he must go in pursuit of Rama, and persuade him to return and assume the sovereignty. The meeting between the brothers shows the utmost delicacy and generosity of feeling; Bharata lamenting his mother's ill conduct, and entreating Rama to return; Rama declining because unless he keeps his father's vow he cannot secure his father's happiness in heaven: he therefore adjures his brother to return to Ayodhya and "console the people and the twice-born. I with Sita and Lakshman will enter the forest of Dandaka. Be thou the King of men, I will be sovereign of wild beasts. Let the umbrella shade thy head, I will take refuge in the shade of the wood."—MRS. SPEIR, *Life in Ancient India.*

" Urge me no more: thy words are fair,
But virtue's garb they falsely wear.
With pleasing art thy tongue misleads,
And lures me to ignoble deeds.
For what is might or ancient race,
The pomp of wealth, the pride of place?
'Tis virtue marks the line between
The great and good, the low and mean:
And he from virtue's path who strays,
To wander in forbidden ways,
Whate'er his birth, must hope in vain
The praises of the good to gain.

Shall I the righteous path forsake,
The laws of duty foully break;
Be scorned by all the good and just,
And lay mine honour in the dust?
Shall Rama stain his soul with sin,
And lose the heaven he lives to win?
Nor would the crime with Rama end:
For countless lives on him depend.
The people in their prince behold
Their best example, guide, and mould,
And, by his vice or virtue led,
The path he walks they strive to tread.
That truth and mercy still must be
Beloved of kings, is Heaven's decree
Upheld by truth the monarch reigns
Nay, truth the very world sustains.
Truth evermore has been the love
Of saints below and Gods above;
And endless bliss by truth is won
In Brahma's world beyond the sun.
For holy truth is root and spring
Of virtue and each lovely thing:
A mighty Lord, supreme on earth,
Peerless for beauty, power, and worth:
A crown of glory, still more fair
Than sacrifice and praise and prayer.
Shall I this heavenly gem despise,
Attracted by an earthly prize?
Shall I, misled by lust of sway,
My father's order disobey;

And, folly's dupe or passion's slave,
Force him to break the oath he gave?
Shall I, to gain my royal right,
The clear command of duty slight:
With lying lips my glory stain,
And basely sin for paltry gain?
For not alone by hand and thought
The soul of man with crime is fraught:
Sin's meanest tool I count the third,
The tongue that speaks the lying word.
No, brother; urge this plea no more,
I still will keep the oath I swore:
Within the forest calmly dwell,
Contented with my hermit's cell,
Nor fail to give the Gods a share
Of offerings from my humble fare."

THE FOREST.

"Though reft of power and kingly sway,
Though friends and home are far away,
I cannot mourn my altered lot,
Enraptured with this lovely spot.
Look, darling, on this noble hill,
Which sweet birds with their music fill
Tinged with a thousand metal dyes,
His lofty summits kiss the skies.
Here gleams a line of silvery sheen,
There, a broad streak of emerald green;
And, next, a belt of gold is spread,
Made glorious by a fringe of red;
While, higher as the peaks ascend,
Sunlight and flowers and crystal blend.
See, dear, the trees that clothe his side,
All lovely in their summer pride,
In richest wealth of leaves arrayed,
With flower and fruit and light and shade.
Look where the young rose-apple glows:
What loaded boughs the mango shows!
See, waving in the western wind,
The light leaves of the tamarind;

And mark that giant peepul through
Those feathery clumps of tall bamboo.
That depth of shade, that open lawn,
Allure the wood-nymph and the faun
And, where those grassy glades extend,
The spirits of the air descend
To while the summer night away
With dalliance and mirth and play.
Look, from the mountain's woody head
Hangs many a stream like silver thread,
Till, gathering strength, each rapid rill
Leaps, lightly laughing, down the hill;
Then, bounding o'er the rocky wall,
Flashes the foamy water-fall.
O, lives there one too cold to feel
Delicious languor o'er him steal,
As the young morning breeze, that springs
From the cool cave on balmy wings,
Breathes round him, loaded with the scent
Of bud and blossom, dew-besprent!
See, round the hill, at random thrown,
Those masses of primeval stone,
Of every shape and many a hue,
Yellow and black and red and blue.
But all is fairer still by night:
Each rock reflects a softer light,
When the whole mount, from foot to crest,
In robes of lambent flame is drest;
When, from a million herbs, a blaze
Of their own luminous glory plays,

And, clothed in fire, each deep ravine,
Each pinnacle and crag is seen.
Dear Sita, Chitrakuta's height
Transports me with such pure delight,
With thee and Lakshman here to dwell
For many a year would please me well."
" Home of the heron and the swan
See, the fair river glides,
With verdant isles to gem her breast,
And flowers to deck her sides.
With every tree of sweetest fruit
And fairest bloom that springs ;
And glorious as the lucid stream
Where bathes the King of Kings.[1]
How lovely are those shelving banks,
Now dotted o'er with deer,
That sully, as they quench their thirst,
The waves that were so clear.
Look, darling, to that point below,
Those holy hermits mark,
I know them by their matted hair,
And by their coats of bark.
See, on the river bank they stand,
Their early bathing done ;
Lifting their aged hands in prayer
They reverence the sun.
O look, the merry wind is up,
And scatters leaves around :

[1] A title of Kubera, the God of Wealth. The beauty of his pleasure-grounds is proverbial.

The very mountain seems to dance
  With bending forests crowned.
Behold the wavelets white with foam
  As round the isles they whirl;
Here troubled by the bathing saints,
  And there like orient pearl.
Look, scattered by the morning breeze,
  What beds of blossoms lie,
And chaplets, cast upon the wave,
  Are dancing swiftly by.
Hark to the wild-duck's merry call,
  Amid the reeds at play:
Hark to the joyous mallard's note
  Responsive far away.
My life in fair Ayodhya's town
  Was not so sweet to me
As gazing on this lovely flood,
  That glorious hill, and thee.
Bathe in the gentle stream, to her,
  With friendly love, repair,
And pluck her lilies in thy play,
  And twine them in thy hair.
This mount, with all its savage life,
  Ayodhya's city deem,
And on this beauteous river look
  As our own Sarju's stream.
O Sita, I am wild with joy,
  So rare a lot is mine—
Cheered by a duteous brother's care,
  And loved with love like thine."

THE RAPE OF SITA.

"Ravana, finding it in vain to hope to succeed without the aid of stratagem, took with him an assistant sorcerer, disguised as a deer; and as Rama took great pleasure in the chase, it was not difficult for the deer to lure him from his cottage in pursuit. He did not leave his beloved Sita without charging Lakshman, his brother, to remain in charge; but the wily deer knew how to defeat his precaution, and when transfixed by Rama's arrow he cried out in the voice of Rama, 'Oh, Lakshman, save me!' Sita heard the cry, and entreated Lakshman to fly to his brother's rescue. He was unwilling to go, but yielded to her earnestness and she was left alone."—MRS. SPEIR, *Life in Ancient India.*

As, when the sun and moon their empire leave,
Black night descends upon the widowed eve;
So Ravan, watching for the lovely prize—
His form concealed in roaming Brahman's guise—
Drew near to Sita, in the cottage left,
Far from her guardians, of all aid bereft.
All life was husht, and, as the fiend came near,
No leaflet stirred, the wind was still through fear;
And his red eye held, powerless to flee,
The trembling waters of Godaveri.
Unholy guest in holy guise he came,
Close to the side of Rama's mourning dame:
Like a dark well with treacherous weeds o'ergrown,
Like Saturn when his baleful rays are thrown
Upon the fairest star of all the sky,
Thus the Night-rover with his evil eye

Looked on the lonely lady as she wept
Within her leafy home. Awhile he kept
His gaze upon her beauty, for it fed
Upon the splendour of white teeth, the red
Of luscious lips, the light of eyes that through
Their long soft lashes, moistened with the dew
Of weeping, glorified a face, fair-browed,
Pure as the moon shining without a cloud.

Then Ravan cried, pierced by Love's fiery dart:
"Speak, marvellous beauty, tell me who thou art:
All lonely here, in silken robes arrayed,
Wearing a lotus wreath thy brows to shade:
What heavenly being do mine eyes behold,
Fairer and brighter than the finest gold?
Fame? Beauty? Modesty?—No less I ween,
Or sweet Desire young Love's voluptuous queen?
Red are thy lips, thy teeth are small and white;
Thy tender eyes are large and soft and bright.
No child of earth could wear a smile so sweet,
And O, the wonder of thy perfect feet!
Robes cannot hide the glories of thy breast,
And fancy faintly pictures all the rest.
Sweet queen, these eyes have never seen till now
Sylph, nymph, or Goddess half so fair as thou.
This savage wood befits thee, lady, ill,
Where wild fiends roam, changing their form at will.
On some smooth terrace should thy couch be spread,
In gardens sweet with blooms thy feet should tread;
A royal robe thy peerless form should deck,
And priceless gems sparkle upon thy neck;

The choicest wreath should bind thy glorious hair,
A matchless lord thy bed of love should share.
Who art thou, Goddess ? but no heavenly maid
Loves this wild wood : beneath this gloomy shade
No nymph or gentle spirit seeks to roam ;
This is the giant's haunt, the lion's home.
Dost thou not dread, so delicate and fair,
The tiger near thee and the wolf and bear ?
Whose and who art thou ? Tell me, whence and why
Thou comest hither, with no guardian nigh."

He ceased. The lady, by his garb beguiled,
With fearless innocence lookèd up and smiled ;
She bade the seeming Brahman to a seat,
And gave him water for his weary feet ;
And, still intent on hospitable care,
Brought forth the choicest of her woodland fare.
She by the cottage-door expecting stood
To see her lord returning through the wood ;
But naught save boundless trees her gazes met :
Rama and Lakshman, lingering, came not yet.
And then she told him what he sought to know,
Her name, her lineage, all her weal and woe :
The monarch's promise, and Kaikeyi's hate,
The fatal oath, and grief that came too late.
" And now," she said, " declare thy name and race,
And why thou roamest to this gloomy place."

She spoke. The stranger thundered in reply :
Terror of men and Gods and worlds am I,
Ravan, whose will the giant hosts obey.

Since I have seen thee, lovely one, to-day,
Clad in silk raiment, bright as polisht gold,
My love for all my wives is dead and cold.
Though countless dames of perfect beauty, torn
From many a pillaged realm, my home adorn,
Come, fairest, come, my queen and darling be;
Among a thousand I will love but thee.
My city, Lanka, like a glittering crown,
Looks from the high brow of a mountain down
On restless Ocean, who with flash and foam
Beats in wild rage against my island-home.
There pleasant gardens shall thy steps invite
With me to wander when the moon is bright;
There in new joys thy breast shall ne'er retain
One faint remembrance of this place of pain."

Then from her breast the noble fury broke;
With flashing eye and quivering lip she spoke:
"Me, me, the faithful wife of Rama, him
Before whose glory Indra's fame is dim:
Rama, who quails not in the battle-shock,
Fierce as the Ocean, steadfast as the rock
Rama, the lord of each auspicious sign;
Rama, the glory of his princely line;
Me, Rama's wife, the dear fond wife of him,
Him of the eagle eye, the lordly limb—
Me dost thou dare with words of love to press,
A jackal suing to a lioness?
As far above thine impious reach am I
As yonder sun that blazes in the sky.

Ha! thou hast seen those air-drawn trees of gold,
That sign of doom which dying eyes behold,
If thou hast ventured, weary of thy life,
To look with eyes of love on Rama's wife.
Fool! thou hadst better strive to rend away
The serpent's venomed fang, the lion's prey;
To steal the blessed tree that blooms on high,
To drink fell poison and not fear to die.
Fool! with a needle's point thine eye to prick;
Fool! with thy tongue a razor's edge to lick.
Thou, tempt the wife of Rama! Better leap,
A millstone round thy neck, from Lanka's steep
Into the raging sea and strive to swim
From shore to shore than tempt the wife of him.
Thou, win his wife! With lighter labour try
To pluck the sun and moon from yonder sky;
Safer to wrap within thy robe the flame,
Than woo to folly Rama's faithful dame.
As the vast ocean to a trickling rill,
As Meru's mountain to the meanest hill;
The feathered monarch to the skulking bat,
The lordly lion to the crawling cat:
As sandal perfume to the common mire;
As gold, found perfect by the testing fire,
To homely iron and dull lumps of lead:
As the gay peacock, with his plumes outspread,
To the shy moping solitary owl:
As the proud swan is to the meanest fowl
That dips his wings, unnoticed, in the sea—
So is my Rama to a thing like thee."

Out burst the giant, with a furious frown:
" Hast thou not heard of Ravan's high renown?
Ne'er heard the glory and the might of me
Before whose face celestial armies flee?
Whom all the Gods, with Indra at their head,
Fear like the ruthless Monarch of the Dead;
Before whose eye the sun and moon grow pale,
And silent horror checks the shuddering gale;
That every leaflet on the tree is still,
Husht every ripple of the babbling rill.
Beyond the sea my glorious city stands,
Lanka the famous, raised by giant hands:
Like Indra's city, beautiful and bright
With golden walls and gates of lazulite.
There every flower of rarest odour blows,
And luscious fruit on loaded branches glows;
There is the sound of cymbal and of drum:
Tarry not, Sita, but arise and come!
Come, and with me all earthly pleasures share;
Nay, heavenly joys, my love, shall bless thee there."

He ceased; and, changing all his gentle guise,
Stood before Sita in his native size,
A monstrous giant, terrible in form,
Dark as a thunder-cloud that leads the storm.
Ten-faced and twenty-armed, in every head
Glared the wild eye-balls that his rage made red,
As with a scowl upon each haughty brow,
He cried: " Fair Sita, wilt thou scorn me now?
Lift thy sweet eyes, dear child of earth, and see
A husband worthy of a queen like thee."

One eager hand her glorious tresses graspt,
One mighty arm around her waist was claspt;
Aid her, ye Spirits! Ah, all wild with dread
Each nymph and faun before the fiend had fled:
Where, where is Rama? Rama roams afar,
And Ravan bears her to his magic car.

With angry threats the giant tried to still
Her cries for aid, but very long and shrill
Rang forth her lamentation through the air,
As of one raving in her great despair:
"Help, Rama, help! O Lakshman, where art thou?
Why, faithful champion, art thou heedless now?
My hero, wont the giants' pride to tame,
Tear from their impious hands thy brother's dame!
She who drove Rama from his promised throne
Will doubly triumph when this deed is known.
Ye happy bowers, ye bloomy groves, farewell!
My mournful fate to royal Rama tell!
And thou Godaveri, dear stream, upon
Whose bosom float the mallard and the swan,
Forget not her who loves thee, but relate
To royal Rama Sita's mournful fate.
Ye gentle fauns to whom this wood is dear,
Let Rama from your airy voices hear
That Ravan tears me hence! On you, on all
The countless life within these shades I call:
Say that the fiend has borne away his wife,
His own true Sita, dearer than his life;
He will regain the spouse he loves so well,
Yea, if they bore her to the depths of Hell."

Down to her feet her loosend tresses hung,
As, like a creeper, with twined arms she clung
To bough and branch, and, falling on her knees,
Shrieked out for succour to the mighty trees.
Then Ravan's giant hand, unused to spare,
Seized her again by her long flowing hair:
Vengeance on thee that cursed touch shall bring,
And stain with gore thy hair, thou impious king.
All nature trembled, faint and sick with dread,
And sudden darkness o'er the world was spread;
The wind was husht, dimmed was the glorious sun;
An awful voice that cried, The deed is done,
Burst from the mighty Sire, whose sleepless eye
Saw the fell outrage from his throne on high;
And the pure saints, with mingled joy and awe,
Looked on the sinner and his doom foresaw.
In vain she struggled, as the giant threw
His arm around her waist and upward flew.
With yellow robes, far floating uncontrolled,
And fair limbs glowing like the burnisht gold,
The royal lady like the lightning shone,
Too dazzling lovely to be looked upon.
Toucht by the glorious light the giant's frame
Showed like a mountain belted round with flame;
And from the lotus wreath that crowned her head
Light falling petals on his limbs were shed.
Widowed of Rama and of joy, her face
Peered in its lovely sadness from the embrace
Of her fell ravisher. So looks the moon
With pure light cleaving a dark cloud in June.

RAMA'S DESPAIR.

Rama returns to his cottage and finds it empty. Sita, his love, his life, is gone. He had borne the loss of father, mother, home, and friends, but beneath this shock the hero's reason gives way.

Then Rama turning, with love-quickened pace,
Eager to look upon his Sita's face,
Came to his dwelling. But he found her not;
Lonely and empty was the leafy cot,
Like a sad streamlet in the winter's frost
With all the glory of its lilies lost.
He searcht, he called: no answering voice was heard,
But a faint shudder that the branches stirred;
And sad with woe each tree and bird and flower
Mourned round the ruin of the lady's bower;
And nymph and faun in shady thickets sighed.

And Rama lifted up his voice and cried:
"Where is my darling? Dead, or torn away,
Or has she venturned in the wood to stray
Gathering flowers farther and farther still?
Or has she sought the stream, her jar to fill?"
Through grove and glade he ran with maddened brain,
Seeking her wildly where all search was vain.
From brook to brook, from hill to hill he ran,
Each tree to question and each lawn to scan:
"Tell me, Acacia, has that fairest she,
Who loved thy flowers so well, been seen by thee?

Clad in pale silk and like thy clusters, fair,
If thou hast seen my darling, tell me where!
Thou Bel tree, laden with thy golden fruit
Round as my lady's breast, why art thou mute?
Where is she, Heartsease? 'Tis thy gentle part
To banish woe, come give me what thou art.
Thou Cassia, brilliant with thy pendent gold,
Tell me what shades my radiant Sita hold.
Palm, Mango, Jasmine, Amaranth, declare,
Where is my darling with the long soft hair?
It may be that my fawn-eyed love has strayed
To sport with fawns beneath some arching shade.
I see thee, dearest: come, no longer seek
To hide thee in the grove; come forth or speak!
I see thee, lady of the lotus eye,
Thou art not hidden, and 'tis vain to fly.
Stay if thou lovest me, my Sita, stay!
Too much already of this cruel play.
I see thy garment shimmer in the brake:
Stay, my sweet darling, for dear pity's sake!
Why art thou angry? Have I done thee wrong?
O, come, my love, for I have sought thee long!

Ah! she is dead; her mangled limbs the feast
Of wandering giant or some ravenous beast;
That moon-bright cheek, that pure and polisht brow,
Red lips and dazzling teeth—what are they now?
Tossing her arms—her spray-soft arm—in vain,
Shrieking for help, alas! my love was slain.
Why wast thou left within thy bower alone,
For fiends to rend thee, oh, mine own, mine own

My Sita lost, I will not live, but go
Hence to the after-world, weighed down by woe
The mighty king, our sire, will see me there,
And sternly cry, 'False, perjured Rama, where,
Where is thy faith, that thou, with evil speed,
Comest from exile ere the time decreed?'
Can I return from banishment to see
Those chambers empty where my queen should be?
Can I return to hear my people cry
Shame on the wretch who failed to save or die?
How can I meet Videha's king, and brook
The speechless agony of the father's look?
How will these lips endure to tell him all?
These eyes, to see him start and faint and fall?
Now leave me here to mourn awhile and die:
Do thou, dear brother, to Ayodhya hie,
The beautiful city: thus to Bharat say,
With tender greeting: 'Rama bids thee sway
The righteous sceptre thou deservest well.'
Then, after reverent salutation, tell
With soothing words, my mother, his, and thine,
The mournful tale of Sita's fate and mine."

RAMA IN THE SPRING.

'I sought thee there,
And, mourning for my darling scarce could bear
The sweet cool smell of lakes and pleasant showers,
The beauty and the perfume of the flowers,
And all delights of sight, and sound, and smell;
For, without Sita, Heaven itself were Hell.'

—KALIDASA.

Look, brother at that grove,' he cried,
'That lines sweet Pampa's shelving side.
Those trees of giant girth that rear
Their heads so high, like hills appear.
These are the pleasant days that fire
The youthful bosom with desire;
When soft winds, breathing balm, dispense
Wood odours that enthral the sense,
And pour a ceaseless rain of flowers
As drops the cloud his summer showers.
Look, even as I speak, my head
Is covered with the blooms they shed.
How soft the west wind moves along
To music of the wild bee's song;
His breath is of the woodland spring
The sandal's odour lades his wing.
Look up, there hardly glimmers through
These arching trees one speck of blue.

Look there, the Cassia's bloom behold,
A giant clad in burning gold.
O happy spring, whom birds rejoice
To welcome with their gladdest voice!
O happy time, but not to me,
For I am wandering far from thee,
My darling of the large soft eye.
That Koil with his loud shrill cry
Of joy and freedom and desire
That the first days of spring inspire,
Seems calling, as he cheers his mate,
To me all lone and desolate.
See, where the joyous mallard leads
His partner through that fringe of reeds.
Each happy bird, and none alone,
Hails the spring air with gladdest tone,
All revelling in bliss alike,
The swan, the hawk, the dove, the shrike.
Look, brother, in that shady glen
The peacock dances round his hen:
No Giant's hand has reft away
The mate with whom he loves to play.
There, round the Mango blossom, press
Wild bees, with lovers' eagerness.
But ah! the blissful life around,
Each lovely sight, each pleasant sound,
Pierces my very heart, and slays
With memory of perished days.
That flew in heavenly rapture by
With Sita of the roe-deer's eye!'

TIDINGS OF SITA.

The tidings of Sita's abduction by Ravana was brought to Rama by Jatayu, a celestial bird who in a fruitless encounter to snatch Sita away from the ruthless hands of the King of Rakshasas lost his life.

'As on the breezy hill I stood,
That rises o'er the pathless wood,
High o'er me flew a monstrous form,
Dark as the cloud that heralds storm.
I saw the giant's flashing eye;
I heard a woman's piteous cry.
A voice from out the still air came
Of weeping mixt with Rama's name.
A dove, whom eagle talons grasp,
She struggled in the giant's clasp.
I heard again a wilder shriek:
She saw me on the mountain peak.
An anklet from her foot she drew,
And with it cast her garland too.
The token I have guarded well
Some tidings of thy love may tell.'

Quick to the mountain cave he went,
And brought the treasured ornament.
Then burst the tear from Rama's eyes
As, gazing on the well-known prize,
O Sita, O my love !' he said;
Then swooned and fell as fall the dead.

TARA'S LAMENT.

At Jatayu's advice Rama sought the aid of Sugriva, the banished brother of Bâli, the King of Kiskindha and husband of Tara. Rama, accordingly, met Sugriva, asked his help and in return promised to kill Bâli and instal Sugriva in his stead. Rama killed Bali clandestinely and in a manner which was against all the laws of war as understood in ancient India. The following scene describes Tara with her son Angada lamenting beside her deceased spouse Bâli.

Tara, widowed of her spouse,
Kissed him on the cheek and brows ;
O'er her fallen hero bent,
Called him with this wild lament :
'Still, my lord, without reply ?
Is the earth more loved than I,
That thou choosest to recline
On her breast, forsaking mine ?
Lord and keeper, good and brave,
Sage to guide and strong to save,
See, thy chiefs, a mournful ring,
Wait around their silent king.
Wilt thou still be stern and mute ?
Must they miss thy kind salute ?
Dearest, when the morning's red
Calls thee from thy royal bed,
'Tis thy wont to welcome each
With a gift or pleasant speech.
Must thy lords unheeded stay ?
Wilt thou not arise to-day ?
Wilt thou not awake from sleep
While thy friends around thee weep ?

Look, thy child before thee stands;
Lifts to thee his little hands.
Wilt thou, silent yet, despise
That appeal of wistful eyes?
Ah! my love is dead, is dead.
Look ye, how his wounds have bled;
How the crimson torrents make
Round his limbs a rising lake.
Death, my child, has hurried hence
Him who was our sure defence.
Come, and look on him who thus
Slain in fight has gone from us.
Kiss thy sire and say farewell!'
Came the little child and fell
On his knees and fondly pressed
Those cold feet with arm and breast:
'Here is Angada,' he cried;
'Father, speak!' but none replied.
Weeping, as her child she viewed,
Tara thus her plaint renewed:
'Hast thou not a word—not one—
Father, for thy darling son?
Canst thou still and silent lie,
Hear him call, and not reply?
Husband, by thy bloody bed,
Thus I sit and mourn thee dead:
Like some mother of the herd,
By the lion undeterred,
Mourning in the grassy dell
Where her lord and leader fell.'

RAVAN'S PALACE.

Then sweetly to his ear were borne
The blended notes of drum and horn,
Cymbal and tabour, deep and loud,
Like thunder from a distant cloud.
Awhile he stood, then nearer drew,
Till flashed upon his startled view
The car of Ravan, long and wide,
A measured league from side to side :
The car that flew o'er flood and hill
Obedient to the master's will.
Its jewelled arches high o'erhead
An ever-changing lustre shed
From ruby, pearl, and every gem,
On golden pillars under them.
Delicious came the tempered air
That breathed a heavenly summer there,
Stealing through bloomy trees that bore
Each pleasant fruit in endless store :
Enclosed within that pearly bound,
The wondering chief a palace found,
Of vast extent and stately height
With doors of gold and lazulite,
And decked with every lovely thing,
The mansion of the Giant King.
No check was there from jealous guard,
No door was fast, no portal barred.

Only a sweet air breathed to meet
The stranger, as a host should greet
A wanderer of his kith and kin
And woo his weary steps within.
He stood within a spacious hall
With fretted roof and painted wall,
The giant Ravan's boast and pride,
Loved even as a lovely bride.
'Twere long to tell each marvel there,
The crystal floor, the jewelled stair,
The gold, the silver, and the shine
Of chrysolite and almandine.
There breathed the fairest blooms of spring,
There flashed the proud swan's silver wing,
The splendour of whose feathers broke
Through fragrant wreaths of aloe smoke.
''Tis India's heaven,' the chieftain cried,
Gazing in joy from side to side:
'The home of all the Gods is this:
The mansion of eternal bliss!'
There were the softest carpets spread,
Delightful to the sight and tread,
Where troops of fairest women lay
O'ercome by sleep, fatigued with play.
The cup no longer cheered the feast;
The sound of revelry had ceased;
The tinkling feet no longer stirred;
No chiming of a zone was heard.
So when each bird has sought her nest,
And swans are mute and wild bees rest,

Sleep the fair daughters of the lake
Till the sun's kiss shall bid them wake.
Like the calm field of autumn's sky
Which stars unnumbered glorify,
So shone the tyrant's sumptuous room
With living stars that chased the gloom.
'These are the stars,' the chieftain cried,
'In summer nights that earthward glide;
In brighter form they re-appear
To shine in matchless lustre here.'

With wondering eyes awhile he viewed
Each graceful form and attitude.
One lady's head was backward thrown,
Bare was her arm and loosed her zone.
The garland that her brow had graced
Hung closely round another's waist.
Here gleamed two little feet, all bare
Of anklets that had sparkled there.
Here lay a queenly dame at rest
In all her glorious garments dressed.
There slept another whose small hand
Had loosened every tie and band.
In careless grace another lay
With gems and jewels cast away,
Like a young creeper when the tread
Of the wild elephant has spread
Destruction and confusion round,
And hurled it flowerless to the ground.
Here lay a slumberer still as death,
Save only that her balmy breath

Raised ever and anon the lace
That floated o'er her sleeping face.
There, sunk in sleep, an amorous maid
Her sweet head on a mirror laid,
Like a fair lily bending till
Her petals float upon the rill.
Another black-eyed damsel pressed
Her lute upon her heaving breast,
As though her happy arms were twined
Round him for whom she long had pined.
Another pretty sleeper round
A silver vase her arms had wound,
That seemed—so fresh and fair and young—
A wreath of flowers that o'er it hung.

In sweet disorder lay a throng
Weary of dance and play and song :
Where heedless girls had sunk to rest,
One pillowed on another's breast,
Her tender cheek scarce seen beneath
Red roses of the falling wreath,
The while her long soft hair concealed
The beauties that her friend revealed.
With limbs at random interlaced
Round arm and leg and throat and waist,
That wreath of women lay asleep
Like blossoms in a careless heap.

SITA IN PRISON.

As some poor solitary deer,
When eager dogs are pressing near,
Lies sobbing in an alien wood
Far from her soft-eyed sisterhood;
So in King Ravan's hall a prey
To fear and anguish, Sita lay,
With none to aid her in distress,
Girt round by many a giantess.

Pierced by the shaft of Love, the King
Strode to the centre of the ring.
He bade the captive lady rise,
And, lifting up her streaming eyes,
View all the glorious house that vied
With heavenly homes in pomp and pride:
Hall, bower, and chamber, bright with throngs
Of gay-robed dames and cheered with songs
Of countless birds whose swelling throats
Blent sweetly their delicious notes
From gold and crystal pillars bright
With studs of pearl and lazulite.
Near lay a royal garden, fair
With terrace, lawn, and gay parterre,
Where roses glowed and peacocks played,
Delighted in the Mango's shade.

Like cloudy pile, in skies of June,
That hides the path of sun and moon;
Or soaring up like Meru's head
All flaming with the morning's red,
So vast, so high that palace raised
Sky-cleaving pinnacles, and blazed
In the sun's path, from floor to spire
A shape of beauty clothed in fire.

He led her up the stairs whereon,
Inlaid in gold, large diamonds shone,
And to her eyes that marked not showed
The glory of his rich abode:
The lattice with its ivory frame,
Where softened light through silver came;
And curtains, bound with golden braid,
Cast on the floor a rosy shade:
The car, obedient to his will,
That bore him over flood and hill:
Long galleries and stately halls
Where pictures lived upon the walls:
The mazy rill that murmured round
The grotto and the pleasure-mound:
Pools where the lily flushed, the lake
Where played the cygnet and the drake.
Thus with delight from view to view,
The undelighted dame he drew.
And as she trembled by his side,
'Look, Sita!' at each step he cried.
'Now, fair one, learn my power and might:
Ten million Rovers of the Night,

And lesser Fiends, a countless band,
Millions of millions round me stand,
Who joy in fight and scorn to fly;
Of all this host sole lord am I.
Whose legions are so vast and bold?
What king so rich in gems and gold?
What earthly city can compare
With Lanka, fairest of the fair?
To thy sweet hand I yield the whole,
O dearer than my life and soul.
Thousands of women wait my sign:
O large-eyed, be their queen and mine.
My earnest prayer no longer spurn,
For Love's hot fires within me burn.
Sea-girt, three hundred leagues in length,
My Lanka lies, and if the strength
Of heavenly hosts her walls assail,
Though Indra lead, their might would fail.
No spirit of the earth or air,
No God can with my strength compare.
No longer let thy fancy dwell
On Rama in his hermit cell;
Leave the poor mortal to his fate,
And wed thee with a worthier mate.
Thy youth will not for ever stay,
Come, use it ere it glide away.
Let no vain hope thy breast beguile
Of rescue from the Giants' isle.
Less vain the toil that sought to tame
The glory of the quenchless flame:

Less vain the toil that strove to bind
The gale that wanders swift as mind.
Man, Fiend or God would find it hard
To rescue thee whom I would guard.
Spurn not, fair queen, a realm like this,
But dwell with me and reign in bliss.
Thy hermit life has washed away
What stain upon thy bright soul lay;
Now come with me enjoy the meed
Of each high thought and noble deed.

What still reluctant, cold, and coy!
Still loving grief and hating joy!
Hear, lady of the faultless brow,
Ravan ne'er stooped so low till now.
Down at thy perfect feet I kneel,
And pity beg for all I feel:
My heads beneath thy feet, I crave
Some mercy for thy loving slave.'

'My large-eyed Rama, dear to fame,
Of mighty arm and lion frame,
And Lakshman, will not tarry long,
But slay thee though thy walls are strong.
Soon will he hurry on thy track,
And with thy life take Sita back.
Small aid 'gainst him thy hosts will bring,
Like snakes seized by the Feathered King,
Though they be terrible and fierce.
The arrows from his bow will pierce

Thy body through, from flank to flank,
As Ganga rends away the bank.
Though girt by hosts of demon shape,
Thou canst not from his hand escape.
Thou, when he holds thee with his eye,
Scorched with his shafts shalt fall and die.
He who can dry the mighty deep
May bid poor Sita moan and weep,
But the great sun shall cease to shine
Ere her pure soul to sin incline.
Repent, ere yet it be too late,
The crime thy death shall expiate,
Or soon shall seas of blood be spilt,
And widowed Lanka mourn thy guilt.
When Rama's shaft has laid thee low,
Far other words thy tongue shall know:
Thou scarcely then wilt boast in pride
That thou hast torn me from his side.
He comes; and 'neath his anger all,
Thyself, thy host, thy town shall fall.
I spurn thee: can the altar dight
With vessels for the sacred rite,
O'er which the priest his prayer has said,
Be sullied by an outcast's tread?
My body lies within thy power:
Torture it, chain it, kill, devour;
Ne'er will I meet thy base desire,
Or lay mine honour in the mire.'

With looks of fury Ravan cried:
'Come, Ogresses, and tame her pride;'

He spoke; and quicker than the word,
The coming of the Fiends was heard.
Shuddered the air as on they sped,
And the earth shook beneath their tread.
Before their lord they humbly bowed,
And pressed round Sita in a crowd.
'To the Asoka-garden bear
My prize,' he cried, 'and guard her there
Until her stubborn pride be bent
By mingled threat and blandishment:
See that ye watch her well, and tame,
Like some wild thing, the haughty dame.'
They bore her to that garden, bright
With every flower that charms the sight,
Where sweet streams under branches flowed,
And fruit through all the seasons glowed.
Prostrate, before those fiendish eyes,
Like a poor trembling deer that lies
Beneath a tiger's paw, she lay
Thinking of Rama far away.

KUMBHAKARNA.

"Kumbhakarna, the gigantic brother of the titanic Ravan,—named from the size of his ears which could contain a *kumbha* or large water-jar—had such an appetite that he used to consume six months' provisions in a single day. Brahma, to relieve the alarm of the world, which had begun to entertain serious apprehensions of being eaten up, decreed that the giant should sleep six months at a time and wake for only one day during which he might consume his six months' allowance without trespassing unduly on the reproductive capabilities of the earth. When Rama invaded the capital of Ravan, the titans requiring all their forces, employed the most violent measures—and eventually with success—to wake the sleeping giant."

With troubled spirit and with broken pride
Through Lanka's gate the vanquisht Ravan hied,
Crusht like an elephant who falls beneath
The lion's spring, and feels the murderous teeth,
Or like a serpent 'neath the furious wing
And vengeful talons of the feathered king.
Such was the giant's fear and wild alarm
At the swift arrows shot by Rama's arm—
Shafts, with the flame of lightning round them curled
Like Brahman's fiery bolts that end the world.
At length, supported on his golden throne,
With failing eye he spoke and humbled tone:
"Alas! ye giants, all the toil is vain,
Fruitless my penance and an age of pain,
If I whom Indra's self confest his peer,
Secure of Gods, a mortal victor fear.

My soul remembers—now, alas! too late—
The words of Brahma which foretold my fate:
'Tremble, proud Giant,' thus the warning ran—
'And fear destruction from unheeded man.
Secure from God and fiend and angel, live,
From faun and serpent, by the boon I give.
Against their power and might thy life is charmed,
Against man only is thy soul unarmed.'
Too well I know the fated hour is nigh:
Then let each leader to his station fly.
Guard every alley with a chosen band,
Let giant warders on the rampart stand,
And let the terror of immortal eyes,
Great Kumbhakarna, from his trance arise.
He in deep slumber, free from care and pain,
Lulled by a charm for many a month has lain.
Let him arise, our bravest, best of all,
And soon the foemen 'neath his arm will fall.'
The giant hosts their monarch's word obeyed,
And left his presence trembling and afraid.
They carried flowery garlands, sweet and fresh,
And, for his banquet, loads of blood and flesh.
They reacht the cavern where the slumberer lay—
A mighty cave that stretcht a league each way:
But scarce the strongest could an entrance gain,
So fierce the tempest as he breathed amain.
They found the giant lying on his bed
With his huge limbs at all their length outspread.
Before his face they piled his favourite cheer,
The flesh of buffaloes and boars and deer.

With garlands, heavenly fair, they fanned his face,
And clouds of incense sweetened all the place.
Then moon-bright conchs they sounded loud and long,
And the cave echoed with the giants' song
Then on their breasts they smote with thundering blows,
And higher yet the wild commotion rose,
When the loud cymbal vied with drum and horn,
And fiendish war-cries on the gale upborne
Through all the air in hideous discord spread,
And the birds heard the din and fell down dead.
But Kumbhakarna calmly took his rest:
And they smote fiercely on his shaggy chest
With maces, clubs, and pieces of the rock,
But still he moved not yet nor felt the shock.
Then all united in one effort more
With shell, drum, tabor, and redoubled roar;
Club, mace, staff, mallet, with strong arms applied,
Rained vigorous blows upon his breast and side;
And screaming elephants were urged to aid,
And beaten camels groaned and horses neighed.
But Kumbhakarna calmly slumbered still.
Then furious wrath began their breasts to fill:
They drencht his forehead with a hundred pails,
They tore his ears and hair with teeth and nails;
They bound together many a murderous mace,
And beat him wildly on the head and face;
And drove wild elephants, with ponderous tread,
Over his mighty limbs and chest and head.
The unusual weight the giant's slumber broke,
He shook his sides and started and awoke;

And, all regardless of the wounds and blows,
Yawning with thirst and faint with hunger, rose.
His jaws like hell gaped terrible and wide,
Red as the sun when glaring o'er the side
Of Meru. Every burning breath he drew
Roared like a mighty wind that rushes through
The cedars on the mountain. Up he raised
His horse-like head, with eyes that fiercely blazed
Like comets; horrible as Death in form
When menacing the worlds with fire and storm.
The giants pointed to the reeking store
Of flesh of buffalo and deer and boar,
And the fiend gorged him with the flesh and blood,
Huge jars of marrow and of wine a flood.
He ended; and the giants ventured near,
And bent their heads in reverence and fear,
And Kumbhakarna looked around with eyes
All glazed and heavy in their first surprize,
And drowsy yet from his late troubled rest
He thus the Rovers of the Night addrest:
"Why have ye called me from my sleep to wake?
None with light cause my rest should dare to break.
Say, is it well with Ravan? Or has need
And fear come on ye, that with heedless speed
Ye thus disturb me? mark the words I say,
The giants' king shall tremble in dismay,
The fire be quencht and Indra's self be slain,
Ere he shall rouse me from my sleep in vain."
The wise Yupaksha humbly thus replied:
"No fiend has dared us, and no God defied.

But gathered men our golden walls assail,
And fear is on us lest their might prevail.
For Rama leads them to the deadly strife,
Burning for vengeance for his ravisht wife.
The hostile flame through Lanka's town has spread,
And Ravan weeps his best and dearest dead.
Nay, e'en our King who never trembled yet
For heavenly hosts or fiends in battle met,
Himself at last the general dread has shared,
By Rama vanquisht and by Rama spared."
Then Kumbhakarna thus in answer spake :
" I will go forth, and deadly vengeance take,
And tread their armies 'neath my conquering feet;
Then, flusht with victory, the King will meet.
The princes' blood shall be my special draught,
By you the gore of all the host be quaffed."

THE DESCENT OF GANGA.

He stood upon the lofty crest
  That crowns the Lord of Snow,
And bade the river of the Blest
  Descend on earth below.

Himalaya's child, adored of all,
  The haughty mandate heard,
And her proud bosom at the call
  With furious wrath was stirred.

Down from her channel in the skies
  With awful might she sped,
In a giant's rush, in a giant's size,
  On Siva's holy head.

'He calls me,' in her wrath she cried
  'And all my flood shall sweep
And whirl him in its whelming tide
  To hell's profoundest deep!'

He held the river on his head,
  And kept her wandering where,
Dense as Himalaya's woods, were spread
  The tangles of his hair.

No way to earth she found, ashamed,
  Though long and sore she strove,
Condemned, until her pride were tamed,
  Amid his locks to rove.

At length when many a year had past
He bade her wanderings end;
Bade the delighted flood at last
Upon the earth descend.

With deafening roar upon the rock
Down sped the heavenly tide,
And earth, who trembled at the shock,
With hollow voice replied.

On countless glittering scales the beam
Of rosy morning flashed,
Where fish and dolphins in the stream,
Fallen and falling, flashed.

Then Bards who chant celestial lays,
And Nymphs of heavenly birth,
Flocked round upon the flood to gaze
That streamed from sky to earth.

The Gods themselves from every sphere,
Incomparably bright,
Borne in their golden cars drew near
To see the wondrous sight.

The cloudless sky was all aflame
With the light of a hundred suns,
Where'er the shining chariots came
That bore those holy ones.

So flashed the air with crested snakes
And fish of every hue,
As when the lightning's glory breaks
Through fields of summer blue.

And white foam-clouds and silver spray
  Were wildly tossed on high,
Like swans that urge their homeward way
  Across the autumn sky.

Now flowed the river calm and clear
  With current deep and strong,
Now slowly broadened to a mere,
  Or scarcely moved along.

Now o'er a length of sandy plain
  Her tranquil course she held:
Now rose her waves and sank again
  By refluent waves repelled.

INGRATITUDE.

O monarch, hear with mind and ear
  The words that Brahma spake.
The thankless man lives under ban;
  Who will, his life may take:
'Man for all sin may pardon win,
  How deep soe'er the guilt;
Yea, for the stain of Brahman slain,
  Whose blood must ne'er be spilt.
Slave to the bowl that kills the soul
  He turns and gains relief;
The liar yet may pardon get,
  The perjured, and the thief.
But never can the thankless man
  Be pardoned for his crime:
Disgrace and shame shall hunt his name
  Through life and endless time.
When, reft of friends, his days he ends
  In profitless remorse,
E'en beasts of prey shall turn away
  And scorn his loathed corse.'

WORKS BY RAI BAHADUR SRIS CHANDRA VASU.

THE ASTADHYAYI OF PANINI

Complete in 1862 pages, Royal Octavo.

Containing Sanskrit Sutras and Vrittis with notes and explanations in English, based on the celebrated Commentary called the Kasika.

PRICE FOR THE COMPLETE WORK.

Indian	**Rs. 45 0 0**
Foreign	**£ 3 0 0**

The Right Hon'ble F. Max Müller, Oxford, 9th February 1892.—"* * * From what I have seen of it it will be a very useful work. What should I have given for such a work forty years ago when I puzzled my head over Pánini's Sutras and the Commentaries. * * I hope you may succeed in finishing your work."

The Right Hon'ble F. Max Müller, Oxford 30th April 1899.—"* * Allow me to congratulate you on your successful termination of Panini's Grammar. It was a great undertaking, and you have done your part of the work most admirably. I say once more what should I have given for such an edition of Panini when I was young, and how much time would it have saved me and others. Whatever people may say, no one knows Sanskrit, who does not know Panini."

Professor T. Jolly, Ph. D. Wurzburg (Germany), 23rd April 1893.—"* * Nothing could have been more gratifying to me no doubt, than to get hold of a trustworthy translation of Panini's Ashtadhyayi, the standard work of Sanskrit literature, and I shall gladly do my best to make this valuable work known to lovers and students of the immortal literature of ancient India in this country."

Professor W. D. Whitney, New Haven, U. S. A., 17th June 1893.—"* * The work seems to me to be very well planned and executed, doing credit to the translator and publisher. It is also, in my opinion, a very valuable undertaking as it does give the European student of the native grammar more help than he can find anywhere else. It ought to have a good sale in Europe (and correspondingly in America.)"

Professor V. Fausboil, Copenhagen, 15th June, 1893.—"* * It appears to me to be a splendid production of Indian industry and scholarship and I value it particularly on account of the extracts from the Kasika."

Professor Dr. R. Pischel, Halle (Saale), 27th May 1893.—"* * I have gone through it and find it an extremely valuable and useful book, all the more so as there are very few Sanskrit scholars in Europe who understand Panini.

PANINI OFFICE, BHUVANESWARI ASRAMA, BAHADURGUNJ, ALLAHABAD.

student of Hindu Law can afford to overlook Mr. Vasu's valuable contribution to the legal literature of the country."

The Hon'ble Mr. Justice Sir N. G. Chandavarkar, Vice-Chancellor of the University of Bombay, writes :—"The translation of the Mitâkṣara is quite faithful to the original and excellent."

The Sacred Books of the Hindus, Vol. III, The Chhandogya Upanisad, translated into English with Madhva's commentary and copious explanatory and critical notes. Cloth, gilt letters, Price Rs. 12.

The Sacred Books of the Hindus, Vol. V, The Vedanta Sutras of Badarayana, translated into English with Govinda Bhâṣya of Baladeva and copious explanatory and critical notes. Cloth, gilt letters, Price Rs. 16.

The *Modern Review* for September 1912, writes :—"An excellent edition of the philosophy."

Siva Sanhita, translated into English. Price 8 As.

An easy Introduction to Yoga Philosophy, Price 8 as.

"Is a very ably written pamphlet by Babu Sris Chandra Vasu, B.A. It is very useful for propaganda work, especially for Bengal and North-Western Provinces. As the price is only one anna, or Rs. 5 per one hundred copies, intending propagandists will do well to distribute this among their friends and respective communities."—*The Theosophy in India.*

Students Edition of the Katha Upanisad. Price 8 as.

The Three Truths of Theosophy. Price 1 anna.

"Is an earnest endeavour to bring the truths of Yoga Philosophy within reach of the general reader; while serving as a convenient hand-book for ready reference for learners and teachers alike."—*The Central Hindu College Magazine, June 1904.*

The right of Wahabis to pray in the same mosque with the Sunnis. An important judgment on a very disputed question of Muhammadan Law. Price Rs. 2.

The Compass of Truth, being the English translation of Risala-i-Haq-numa, by Prince Muhammad Dara Shikoh. Price 8 annas.

[Ready for the Press].

Catechism of Hinduism.

2nd Edition, Revised and Enlarged.

THE IDYLLS FROM THE SANSKRIT

BY

RALPH T. H. GRIFFITH, M.A., C.I.E.,

LATE PRINCIPAL, QUEEN'S COLLEGE, BENARES.

With his portrait and biographical sketch,

BY

MAHAMAHOPADHYAYA
PANDIT ADITYARAM BHATTACHARYA, M.A.

(CLOTH, GILT LETTERS.)

BY THE SAME AUTHOR.

SCENES
FROM
THE RAMAYANA

(CLOTH, GILT LETTERS.)

PANINI OFFICE, BHUVANESWARI ASRAMA, BAHADURGUNJ, ALLAHABAD.

२—प्रथम विभाग प्रथम खण्ड—प्राचीन ग्रीसेर जातीय शिक्षा—

मूल्य १)। कलिकाता विश्वविद्यालयेर अधीनस्थ कालेजसमूहेर इन्स्पेक्टर अध्यापक श्रीयुत विनयेन्द्रनाथ सेन, एम॰ ए॰ कर्तृक लिखित भूमिकासहित। बङ्गीय साहित्य-परिषत् प्रथम संस्करणेर स्वत्वाधिकारी।

३—तृतीय विभाग प्रथम खण्ड—भाषा-शिक्षा, **मूल्य ॥=)**

४—,, ,, द्वितीय खण्ड—संस्कृत-शिक्षा, चारिभागे विभक्त, **मूल्य ३॥)।**

५—,, ,, तृतीय खण्ड—इंराजी॰ शिक्षा, **मूल्य २॥)।**

Extract from the Foreword by Dr. Brajendra Nath Seal, M. A., Ph. D.: "Based on sound and advanced ideas of educational science * * His brochure on the *Study of Language* * * useful summary of present-day ideas on the subject. * * *Lessons on English* and *Sanskrit* are an improvement on existing guides and handbooks. Professor Sarkar's programme is certainly an ambitious one, but he is fully qualified to carry it out, and there is no doubt that it will be found to be a healthy and stimulating force in the Indian educational world of to-day."

Letter from Mahamahopadhyaya Pandit Adityaram Bhattacharya, M. A., Late Professor of Sanskrit Literature, Muir Central College, Fellow, Allahabad University.

"I write this in my appreciation of your effort to facilitate and popularise the study of Sanskrit. Your method to teach Sanskrit without the learner's going through a first course of grammar merits trial.

"The old method has done its part so long and will remain inevitable in the case of higher and thorough study. But if quicker method of acquiring language, living or dead, be discovered and introduced, humanity will bless him whose inventive genius can succeed to achieve the object which every well-wisher of learning has at heart.

"At the very outset the attempt looks somewhat revolutionary. But in other fields it is such revolutionary departures from the old track that has hastened the advance of arts and sciences."

Meghaduta, translated in English verse by S. C. Sarkar, M.A., P. C. S., with critical and explanatory notes, &c. Price—12 annas.

PANINI OFFICE, BHUVANESWARI ASRAMA, BAHADURGUNJ, ALLAHABAD.

The Sacred Books of the Hindus

ALREADY PUBLISHED

Vol I.—Upanisads—The Isa, Kena, Katha, Prasna, Mundaka, and Mandukya Upanisads with Madhva's commentary, translated into English, with copious explanatory notes by Rai Bahadur Srisa Chandra Vasu. Cloth bound, silver letters. Second Edition, Price Rs. 5.

Vol. II.—Yajnavalkya Smriti with the commentary Mitaksara and notes from the gloss of Balambhatti, translated into English with copious explanatory notes by Rai Bahadur Srisa Chandra Vasu. This work is indispensable to all Indian lawyers.

Part I.—Mitaksara with Balambhatti, two chapters.

Price—One Rupee and eight annas. Ditto, Sanskrit Text, Rs. 2.

Vol. III.—The Chhandogya Upanisad with Madhva's Bhasya, translated into English with copious explanatory notes by Rai Bahadur Srisa Chandra Vasu. Cloth bound, gilt letters. Price Rs. 12.

Vol. IV.—Aphorisms of Yoga by Patanjali, with the commentary of Vyasa and the gloss of Vachaspati Misra: by Rama Prasada, M.A., cloth bound, silver letters, Rs. 5.

Vol. V.—The Vedanta Sutras with Baladeva's Commentary translated into English with copious explanatory notes by Rai Bahadur Srisa Chandra Vasu. Cloth, gilt letters. Price Rs. 16.

Vol. VI.—The Vaisesika Sutras of Kanada with the Commentary of Sankara Misra and extracts from the gloss of Jayanarayana. Translated by Nanda Lal Sinha, M.A., B.L. Cloth, silver letters. Price Rs. 7.

Vol. VII.—The Bhakti Sastra, containing Sutras of Narada and Sandilya, and Bhaktiratnavali of Visnu Puri. Translated into English by Nanda Lal Sinha, M.A., B.L., Manmatha Nath Pâl, B.A., B.L., and a retired Professor of Sanskrit respectively. Cloth, gilt letters. Price Rs. 7.

Vol. VIII.—The Nyaya Sutras of Gotama, translated into English with an original Commentary by Mahamahopadhyaya Dr. Satis Chandra Vidyabhusan, M.A., Ph.D., Principal Sanskrit College Calcutta. Part I. Price 1 Re. 8 as.

Vol. IX.—The Garuda Purana translated into English by Earnest Wood. Cloth, gilt letters. Price Rs. 3-8.

Vol. X.—The Mimamsa Sutras of Jaimini, translated into English with an original commentary, by Mahamahopadhyaya Dr. Ganga Nath Jha, M.A., D. Litt. Parts 1, 2 and 3. Price Rs. 4-8.

Vol. XI.—The Samkhya Pravachana Sutra with the Vritti of Aniruddha, and the Bhasya of Vijnana Bhiksu and extracts from the Vritti-Sara of Mahadeva Vedantin, translated by Nandalal Sinha, M.A., B.L., Deputy Magistrate, Bihar. Part I. Price Re. 1, 8 as.

PANINI OFFICE, BHUVANESWARI ASRAMA, BAHADURGUNJ, ALLAHABAD.

THE

Sacred Laws of the Aryas

Professor Jolly in his Tagore Law Lectures says :—

"In modern times, after the establishment of the British rule in India, the hold of the early native institutions over the Indian mind was found to have remained so firm that it was considered expodient to retain the old national system and option amidst the most sweeping changes which had been introduced in the administration of the country and in judicial proceduro. It was the desire to ascertain the authentic opinions of the early nativo legislators in regard to these subjects which led to the discovery of the Sanskrit literature. European Sanskrit philology may be said then to owe a debt of gratitude to the memory of the ancient Sanskrit Lawyers of India."

Sir Henry Sumner Maine says that India

"May yet give us a new science not less valuable than the science of language and folklore. I hesitate to call it comparative jurisprudence, because if it ever exists, its area will be so much wider than the field of law. For India not only contains (or to speak more accurately, did contain) an Aryan language older than any other descendant of the common mother tongue and a variety of names of natural objects less perfectly crystallised than elsewhere into fabulous personages, but it includes a whole world of Aryan institutions, Aryan customs, Aryan laws, Aryan ideas in a far earlier stage of growth and development than any which survive beyond its border."

What Maine hesitated to call comparative jurisprudence cannot be brought into existence unless the legal lore of ancient India is properly studied.

The fact cannot be denied that the contents of the law books of the Hindus are not so well known to Indian legal practitioners unacquainted with Sanskrit as they deserve to be. To remove this want the Pâṇini Office will publish in quarterly parts of 100 royal octavo pages, from October 1912, law books of the Hindus giving original texts, transliteration and translation of every word in the text, together with the translation of authoritative commentaries and such critical and explanatory notes as will elucidate the meaning of the text.

The October number will contain the Prâyaśchitta Adhyâya of Yâjñavalkya Smṛiti with the commentary Mitâkṣara translated into English by Rai Bahadur Śrîśa Chandra Vasu, assisted by Mr. S. N. Naraharayya, of Mysore.

CATALOGUE OF

The Publications of the Panini Office,

BAHADURGANJ, ALLAHABAD,

WHICH AIM AT

"To conserve the ancient learning" of India.—*King-Emperor George V's reply to the Address of the Calcutta University, January 6th, 1912.*

THE SACRED LAWS OF THE ARYAS

OPINIONS OF THE PRESS

The LEADER *of Allahabad writes*:—

In his memorandum on the training of Pandits and Maulvis, submitted to the Conference of Orientalists held at Simla in July last year and published in the official report (recently printed by the Government of India), Rai Sarat Chandra Das Bahadur, C.I.E., the well-known Tibetan scholar and explorer, wrote:—

'It was the administration of Law to Hindus according to their customs and usages which made the judicial officers of the East India Company study Sanskrit. A few works on Hindu Law, *e.g.*, Manu, a portion of the Mitakshara and some others were therefore translated into English. But there are many Hindu law books which are not translated into English and so their contents are not known to those who are not acquainted with Sanskrit. I suggest that the translations of Hindu law books should be undertaken under the supervision of the Hindu Judges of the High Courts in India. Properly qualified European Judges may also help in this work.

'For higher studies in Law where a student takes up Hindu or Mahomedan Law, he should be required to study it from original sources in Sanskrit or Arabic as the case may be. I also suggest that a Chair be established in every Central Law College of a province to teach Hindu and Mahomedan Law. The professors should be scholars of Sanskrit and Arabic. They should be also required to edit and translate law books existing in those languages.'

Sanskrit is a dead language and there are very few scholars in this country or outside it who possess necessary qualifications to undertake the task of critically translating Hindu Law texts. A very thorough knowledge of Sanskrit Grammar is needed for the study of any higher branch of Hindu learning and specially a technical subject like that of Law. We do not know of any one who is better qualified for such a task than Rai Śris Chandra Basu Bahadur * * * He has studied Sanskrit at Benares and produced works which have been spoken of very highly by competent Sanskrit scholars all over the world. * * *

Such a Sanskrit scholar who is as well a trained lawyer and judicial officer is best qualified for the work suggested

[*Continued on page iii. of the cover.*]

WORKS BY RAI BAHADUR SRIS CHANDRA VASU.

THE DAILY PRACTICE OF THE HINDUS

Contains the morning and mid-day duties. 2nd Edition, revised and enlarged.

Price Re. 1-4.

The Central Hindu College Magazine for July 1909, in reviewing this book, writes:—

"This is a valuable and yet easily read book that we can keep on hand, to refresh our minds about the truths underlying the daily practice when custom is blunting the perception of the meaning of the recitations we have been taught to address to the Gods, to the Guru and to the Self. As the author puts it: 'these practices will keep alive in us the memory that we are not only physical beings owing duties to our family, kinsmen, guests and outcasts, as well as to beasts and birds, but that we are spiritual beings as well, owing duties to the various grades of spiritual entities—Pitris, Devas, etc., at the same time we shall learn the laws of health and good living.' We strongly recommend the book to all our readers not yet acquainted with it; therein they may find explanations of points of daily ceremonial that may have puzzled them, for the author is enlightened as well as learned, and we also owe to him translations from the Sanskrit of works of Hindu philosophy."

Dr. Coomaraswamy, in reviewing this work, in the *Ceylon National Review*, wrote:—

"This unpretentious little volume is one of quite remarkable interest and importance. For the first time it is made easy for the outsider to understand, from an actual acquaintance, with the daily ritual of a devout Hindu of the old school, the meaning, the method and the depth of Hindu spiritual culture."

"We strongly recommend this little volume to all interested in mental culture, or who wish to know more of Hinduism as it really is."

WORKS BY RAI BAHADUR SRIS CHANDRA VASU.

IN THE PRESS

FOLK-TALES OF HINDUSTAN

BY

SHAIKH CHILLI.

A new illustrated edition dedicated by permission to His Honour SIR JAMES SCORGIE MESTON, K.C.S.I., &c., Lieutenant-Governor of the United Provinces of Agra and Oudh.

Cloth, gilt letters. Price Rs. 2 only.

The REVIEW OF REVIEWS of London writes:—"Stories of a type that recall the delightful romances of the Arabian Nights."

FOLKLORE of London for June 30th, 1909, in review of this work from the pen of Mr. M. Longworth Dames, I.C.S. (Retd.), writes:—

"The stories are told in good English. *** The stories are excellent examples of the tales of wonder, adventure, and enchantment that circulate throughout the Mohammedan world ***. That town of Janjal Nagari in the Land of Darkness is a sort of Gotham with features suggesting Laputa, and the continuation of extreme folly with philosophical disputation is very effective. The more elaborate stories are all good of their class, and 'The Seven Princes,' 'Vikram and the Faqir,' and 'Prince Mahbub' are well worthy of association with our old favourites from Alif Laila.

"It is to be hoped that Shaikh Chilli will continue his collections, and make known to the world some more gems from his treasure-house."

The PIONEER of 22nd December 1912, in the course of a biographical sketch of the author wrote regarding these stories:—

"Serious scholars are generally known to be devoid of what is called "wit and humour.' But his "Folk-Tales of Hindusthan" shows how cleverly he can wield his pen for writing stories interesting and entertaining to the old and the young alike. * * * We may safely predict that like the Arabian Nights Entertainments, these stories will be eagerly read in ages to come by all classes of people. These have already been translated into Bengali and their translations in some other vernaculars are in course of preparation."

This work has been recommended by the Directors of Public Instruction, United Provinces of Agra and Oudh, Punjab and Central Provinces, as a book suitable for the Libraries of Colleges and High Schools. The Educational Department of Bengal as well as of the Baroda State has purchased copies of this work for the use of the Schools in those territories.

PANINI OFFICE. BHUVANESWARI ASRAMA, BAHADURGUNJ, ALLAHABAD.

WORKS BY RAI BAHADUR SRIS CHANDRA VASU.

The Sacred Books of the Hindus, Vol. I, Isa, Kena, Katha, Prasna, Mundaka and Manduka Upanisads, translated into English with Madhva's commentary and copious explanatory and critical notes. Cloth, Silver letters, Price Rs. 5.

Dr. J. Jolly, Professor of Sanskrit, University of Wurzburg, Bavaria, " * * the translation * * does its author every credit."

The *Indian Mirror*, the well-known oldest daily of Calcutta, in its issue of Saturday, the 18th September, 1909, writes:—

"The Panini Office, Allahabad, is to be congratulated on the production of this sumptuous volume of the six well-known Upanishads which have been published with the original text, Sanskrit-English vocabulary of all the words in the text in their *Pada* form, English translation of the text and Madhva's Commentary, together with copious explanatory notes by the translator, Babu Sris Chandra Vasu, the well-known Sanskrit scholar of European and American reputation. Madhva was the founder of the Dvaita School of the Vedanta philosophy, and it is for the first time that his interpretation of the Upanishads has been made known to the English-reading public. The translation has been excellently made. It is readable and not wooden-legged which unhappily is often the case with translation by European Sanskrit scholars who, moreover, do not thoroughly understand the meaning of Sanskrit phrases. * * * We recommend this new undertaking of the Panini Office to our educated countrymen for patronage, for it is an attempt to make the treasures of Hindu thought buried in Sanskrit, accessible to English-knowing public; and hence it deserves every possible encouragement."

The Sacred Books of the Hindus, Vol, II, Part 1, Yajnavalkya Smriti, with the Commentary, Mitaksara and notes from the gloss Balambhatti; translated into English. Price Re. 1. 8 As.

The Allahabad Law Journal, for December 3rd, 1909, writes:— "It is clear that the work of translation could not have been placed in more capable hands and judging from the first instalment which has been published, we have no hesitation in saying that the work has been very well done. The first part deals with the sources of Hindu Law and the duties of a religious student. The lawyer will find much that is interesting in the first chapter on the sources of law. There is much interesting matter and much food for thought in Mr. Vasu's book and as the translator has taken good care to print the original text (with annotations) of *Yajnavalkya's Smriti* and *Vijñānesvara's* commentary, a student of Sanskrit can easily test the accuracy of the translation. It goes without saying that no serious student of Hindu Law can afford to overlook Mr. Vasu's valuable contribution to the legal literature of the country."

The Hon'ble Justice Sir N. G. Chandavarkar, late Vice-Chancellor of the University of Bombay writes:—"The translation of the Mitākṣara is quite faithful to the original and excellent."

The Sacred Books of the Hindus, Vol. III, The Chhandogya Upanisad, translated into English with Madhva's commentary and copious explanatory and critical notes. Cloth, gilt letters, Price Rs. 12.

The Sacred Books of the Hindus, Vol. V, The Vedanta Sutras of Badarayana, translated into English with Govinda Bhāṣya of Baladeva and copious explanatory and critical notes. Cloth, gilt letters, Price Rs. 16.

The *Modern Review* for September 1912, writes:—"An excellent edition of the philosophy."

Siva Sanhita, translated into English. Price 8 As.

An easy Introduction to Yoga Philosophy, Price 8 as.

"Is an earnest endeavour to bring the truths of Yoga Philosophy within reach of the general reader; while serving as a convenient hand-book for ready reference for learners and teachers alike."—*The Central Hindu College Magazine, June 1904.*

Student's Edition of the Katha Upanisad. Price 8 as.

The Three Truths of Theosophy. Price 1 anna.

"Is a very ably written pamphlet by Babu Sris Chandra Vasu, B.A. It is very useful for propaganda work, especially for Bengal and North-Western Provinces. As the price is only one anna, or Rs. 5 per one hundred copies, intending propagandists will do well to distribute this among their friends and respective communities."—*The Theosophy in India.*

The right of Wahabis to pray in the same mosque with the Sunnis. An important judgment on a very disputed question of Muhammadan Law. Price Rs. 2.

The Compass of Truth, being the English translation of Risala-i-Haq-numa, by Prince Muhammad Dara Shikoh. Price 8 annas.

[Ready for the Press.]

Catechism of Hinduism.

2nd Edition, Revised and Enlarged.

PANINI OFFICE, BHUVANESWARI ASRAMA, BAHADURGUNJ, ALLAHABAD.

THE ENGLISH WORKS OF RAJA RAM MOHAN ROY

With an English translation of Tuhfutul Mutwahhdin (His Arabic-Persian pamphlet.)

This edition also contains some additional letters, an Introduction and illustrations. Cr. 8vo., pages 1008. *Price Rs. 2-8, Postage extra.*

CONTENTS

Biographical Sketch of the Author. Introduction. Translation of an abridgment of the Vedanta. Translation of the Mundakopanishad. Translation of the Kathopanishad. Translation of the Isopanishad. Divine Worship by means of the Gayatri. A Defence of Hindu Theism. A Second Defence of the Monotheistical System of the Vedas. An apology for the Pursuit of Final Beatitude. Religious instructions founded on sacred authorities. The Brahmanical Magazine. Answer of a Hindu, &c. Translation of a Sanskrit Tract on Different Modes of Worship. Humble Suggestions, &c. The Trustdeed of the Brahmo Samaj. Autobiographical Sketch. Introduction, &c. Preliminary Remarks—Brief Sketch of the Ancient and Modern Boundaries and History of India. Questions and Answers on the Judicial System of India. Questions and Answers on the Revenue System of India. A paper on the Revenue System of India. Additional Queries, respecting the condition of India. Appendix. Remarks on Settlement in India by Europeans. Translation of a conference between an Advocate for, and an Opponent of, the practice of Burning Widows Alive; from the original Bengali. A second conference between an Advocate for, and an Opponent of, the practice of Burning Widows Alive. Abstract of the Arguments regarding the Burning of Widows, considered as a Religious Rite. Brief Remarks regarding Modern Encroachments on the Ancient Rights of Females, according to the Hindoo Law of Inheritance. Essay on the Rights of Hindus over Ancestral Property according to the Law of Bengal: Appendix: Hindoo Law of Inheritance. Petition against the Press Regulations: (1) to the Supreme Court, and (2) to the King in Council. A letter to Lord Amherst on English Education. Address to Lord William Bentinck. Anti-Suttee Petition to the House of Commons. The Precepts of Jesus, the Guide to Peace and Happiness. An Appeal to the Christian Public in Defence of the Precepts of Jesus. Final Appeal to the Christian Public in Defence of the Precepts of Jesus. Second Appeal to the Christian Public in Defence of the Precepts of Jesus. A letter on the Prospects of Christianity. The Common Basis of Hindooism and Christianity. A Dialogue between a Missionary, and Three Chinese Converts. Speeches and Letters. Petition to Government against the Resumption of Lakheraj Land. A Present to the Believers in one God. Index.

THE PRIVATE JOURNAL OF THE MARQUESS OF HASTINGS

A VERY INTERESTING WORK

Cloth, Gilt letters, Rs. 3, Postage extra.

OPINIONS

Prof. Jadunath Sarkar, M.A., Premchand Roychand Scholar, writes in the Modern Review:—The Panini Office deserves the thanks of the public for placing before them a reprint of this very interesting work at about a quarter of the price of the original. The paper is fairly thick. The misprints are remarkably few. This candid picture of India ninety-four years ago, has interest not only for the student of history and of manners, but also for the traveller, the *shikari*, and the natural historian, Lord Hastings's notes on animals being of no small value. A very pleasing light is thrown on the great pro-consul's character when we see him strictly enjoining that no harm should be done by his camp-followers to the villagers on the way, almost weeping to see that banana trees had been uprooted and used in lining his route, being visibly touched at the silent but respectful welcome of the crowds of Indians on his return to Calcutta, or breaking down at the inevitable parting from the dear ones who must be sent Home to escape the heat of the land of exile. We see in his dealings with native princes that he was a gentleman above everything else; we wonder that it was left for him to discover that in ruling subject races sympathy is the best policy. Comic touches are not wanting.

The Indian Review.—A great deal of valuable information is to be found in this *Journal*. * * * In all his political dealings in India, His Lordship was actuated by a high sense of duty and morality.

This work has been recommended by the Directors of Public Instruction, Bengal, Eastern Bengal and Assam, United Provinces of Agra and Oudh, and Bombay, for the Libraries of Colleges and Schools. The Director of Public Instruction, Bombay, has been pleased to publish the following notification in "*Indian Education*":—"The Private Journal of the Marquess of Hastings, reprinted by the 'Panini Office', Allahabad, Price Rs. 3 per copy, is recommended as a book suitable for the Libraries of Colleges and High Schools in this Presidency."

(Sd.) W. H. SHARP,

Director of Public Instruction.

PANINI OFFICE, BHUVANESWARI ASRAMA, BAHADURGUNJ, ALLAHABAD.

The Sacred Books of the Hindus

Translated by various Sanskrit Scholars.

Edited by MAJOR B. D. BASU, I.M.S. (retired.)

Professor Max Muller rendered an important service to the cause of comparative theology by the publication of the "Sacred Books of the East." The 40 volumes in that series represent the most important scriptures of the principal nations of Asia. Of these, 21 are translations of Sanskrit works. But still some of the most important sacred books of the Hindus have not been published in that series.

It is the duty of every faithful and true votary of Hinduism to do all that lies in his power to make known the contents of his sacred books to the world at large and to his fellow brethren in faith in India. It is not too much to say that a very large number of English educated Hindus, unacquainted with Sanskrit, possess very little knowledge of their sacred scriptures. So, while the Christian and the Mohammadan are well acquainted with their religious scriptures, the Hindu alone is ignorant of his sacred books.

To remove this want, the Pâṇini Office has been publishing in monthly parts, since July 1909, the original texts of the sacred books together with their English translations.

ORDER FORM.

To

The MANAGER,

Pâṇini Office, Bhuvaneśwari Âśram,

Bahadurganj, Allahabad.

SIR,

Please enlist my name as a subscriber to the *Sacred Books of the Hindus* for one year, and realise the annual subscription of Rs. 12-12-0 (inclusive of postage), by sending me all the numbers published since July, 1912, per V. P. P.

Yours faithfully,

Please write very legibly { *Name*

Address

The Sacred Books of the Hindus

ALREADY PUBLISHED

Vol I.—Upanisads—The Isa, Kena, Katha, Prasna, Mundaka, and Mandukya Upanisads with Madhva's commentary, translated into English, with copious explanatory notes by Rai Bahadur Srisa Chandra Vasu. Cloth bound, silver letters. Second Edition, Price Rs. 5.

Vol. II.—Yajnavalkya Smriti with the commentary Mitaksara and notes from the gloss of Balambhatti, translated into English with copious explanatory notes by Rai Bahadur Srisa Chandra Vasu. This work is indispensable to all Indian lawyers.

Part I.—Mitaksara with Balambhatti, two chapters.

Price—One Rupee and eight annas. Ditto, Sanskrit Text, Rs. 2.

Vol. III.—The Chhandogya Upanisad with Madhva's Bhasya, translated into English with copious explanatory notes by Rai Bahadur Srisa Chandra Vasu. Cloth bound, gilt letters. Price Rs. 12.

Vol. IV.—Aphorisms of Yoga by Patanjali, with the commentary of Vyasa and the gloss of Vachaspati Misra: by Rama Prasada, M.A., cloth bound, silver letters, Rs. 5.

Vol. V.—The Vedanta Sutras with Baladeva's Commentary translated into English with copious explanatory notes by Rai Bahadur Srisa Chandra Vasu. Cloth, gilt letters. Price Rs. 16.

Vol. VI.—The Vaisesika Sutras of Kanada with the Commentary of Sankara Misra and extracts from the gloss of Jayanarayana. Translated by Nanda Lal Sinha, M.A., B.L. Cloth, silver letters. Price Rs. 7.

Vol. VII.—The Bhakti Sastra, containing Sutras of Narad and Sandilya, and Bhaktiratnavali of Visnu Puri. Translated into English by Nanda Lal Sinha, M.A., B.L., Manmatha Nath Pal, B.A. B.L., and a retired Professor of Sanskrit respectively. Cloth, gilt letters. Price Rs. 7.

Vol. VIII.—The Nyaya Sutras of Gotama, translated into English with an original Commentary by Mahamahopadhyaya Dr. Satis Chandra Vidyabhusan, M.A., Ph.D., Principal, Sanskrit College, Calcutta. Part I. Price 1 Re. 8 as.

Vol. IX.—The Garuda Purana translated into English by Earnest Wood. Cloth, gilt letters. Price Rs. 3-8.

Vol. X.—The Mimamsa Sutras of Jaimini, translated into English with an original commentary, by Mahamahopadhyaya Dr. Ganga Nath Jha, M.A., D. Litt. Parts 1, 2 and 3. Price Rs. 4-8.

Vol. XI.—The Samkhya Pravachana Sutra with the Vritti of Aniruddha, and the Bhasya of Vijnana Bhiksu and extracts from the Vritti-Sara of Mahadeva Vedantin, translated by Nandalal Sinha, M.A., B.L., Deputy Magistrate, Bihar. Part I, Price Re. 1. 8 as.

PANINI OFFICE. BHUVANESWARI ASRAMA. BAHADURGUNJ, ALLAHABAD.

Vol. XII.—The Brihajjatakam of Varaha Mihira, with illustrations, translated into English by Swami Vijnananand (Hari Prasanna Chatterjee, B.A., L.C.E.) cloth ; gilt letters. Price Rs. 7.

Vol. XIII—Sukra-Niti, translated by Prof. B. K. Sarkar M.A. Parts 1 and 2. Price Rs. 3.

Vol. XIV. The Bṛihadâraṇyaka Upanisad, with Madhva's commentary translated into English, by Rai Bahadur Srisa Chandra Vasu.

[*In preparation.*]

Extra Volume.—The Adhyatma Ramayana, translated into English by Rai Bahadur Lala Baij Nath. Price Rs. 3.

Dr. J. Jolly, Ph. D., Hon. Litt. D., Oxford, Professor of Sanskrit, University of Wurzburg, Bavaria, writes :—"I take a special interest in this new series of the Sacred Books of the Hindus, trusting that it will be a success such as Max Muller's series of the Sacred Books of the East has been. Yours, I gather, is an essentially patriotic undertaking. It will help to promote the interest in things Indian, in Indian learning and Indian religion, both in your country and in Europe."

OUR PATRONS.

The following Governments and Native States have encouraged the publication of the Sacred Books of the Hindus by subscribing to it :—

(1) The Secretary of State for India.
(2) The Government of India.
(3) The Government of Bengal.
(4) The Government of Madras.
(5) The Government of the United Provinces of Agra and Oudh.
(6) H. H. the Maharaja of Travancore.
(7) H. H. the Maharaja of Mysore.
(8) H. H. the Maharaja of Indore.
(9) H. H. the Maharaja Gaekwar of Baroda.
(10) H. H. the Maharaja of Kolhapur.
(11) H. H. the Maharaja of Jodhpur.
(12) H. H. the Maharaja of Rewah.
(13) H. H. the Maharaja of Benares.
(14) The University of Calcutta.
(15) The University of Madras.

etc., etc., etc.

PANINI OFFICE, BHUVANESWARI ASRAMA, BAHADURGUNJ, ALLAHABAD.

read a nation's literature and, above all, its poetry and folk-lore, in which is enshrined that which moves and inspires its heart and soul, with sympathy and an honest endeavour to understand and appreciate, inevitably brings men into closer relation with that nation's life and spirit and so helps to promote Brotherhood. This, one ventures to think, may have been one of the motives which prompted Mr. Griffith to devote so much of his valuable time to these translations—not the least of many services he rendered to India, causing friends and pupils to hold his memory in grateful veneration."

The **Modern Review** *for February 1913, writes* :—

Time was when Sanskrit was not regarded as fit to be compared with Greek and Latin in regard to literary excellence and its philological aspect was alone considered as deserving of study. This was the view placed before the Public Service Commission of 1886 by many cultured Anglo-Indian witnesses who wanted to justify the difference observed by the Indian Civil Service Commissioners in marking the classical languages of the East and the West. No one with any pretensions to culture would, we trust, hold by the same principle now. Not a year passes by but important discoveries are made of works in the Sanskrit language covering the entire domain of human knowledge. Even the oft quoted anonymous verses—the number of which is legion—which fly about from mouth to mouth are found to contain the very quintessence of wisdom, crystalising as they do the generalised experience of an ancient race which has thought deeply on all varieties of subjects affecting human life and conduct. The two neatly got-up volumes before us should serve to dispel the illusion that Sanskrit cannot contribute much to literary culture. Mr. Griffith was himself a poet of no mean order, and he combined with his poetic gift a deep knowledge of, and an abiding love for Sanskrit literature. His free metrical renderings of selected passages have caught the fine spirit of the original in a higher degree than many laboured literary translations. By readers unacquainted with the rich storehouse of Sanskrit literature, or even those who are on the threshold of it, these volumes will be highly appreciated. The publishers have rendered a patriotic service by making available the treasures of Sanskrit literature to foreign readers in their present attractive poetic garb.

The **Hindusthan Review** *for December 1912, writes* :—

The Panini Office (Allahabad) deserve well of admirers of Sanskrit literature by their reprints of the late Mr. Ralph Griffith's *Scenes from the Ramayana* and *Idylls from the Sanskrit.* The latter now includes all Mr. Griffith's fugitive translations from Sanskrit and its value is enhanced by a sketch of the author from the pen of Mahamahopadhyaya Pandit Adityaram Bhattacharya, M.A., as also by a halftone photo of his.

PANINI OFFICE. BHUVANESWARI ASRAMA, BAHADURGUNJ, ALLAHABAD.

WORKS BY

Prof. BENOY KUMAR SARKAR, M.A.

I. **Published by Messrs. Longmans, Green & Co. in London.**—The Science of History and the Hope of Mankind.

II. **TRANSLATION OF PROF. SARKAR'S Works :**—

1. **English** (In the Press in England)—(i) Introduction to the Science of Education. (ii) Lessons on Sanskrit.

2. **Hindi**—(i) National Education in Ancient Greece (In the Press). (ii) The Man of Letters (Sahitya-Sevi). (iii) The Study of Language (In the Press). (iv) Lessons on Sanskrit (In the Press). (v) Introduction to the Science of Education. (vi) The Propagation of Hindu Literature.

III. **IN THE PRESS :**—1. **Sukraniti**—Sukracharyya's System of Morals (Social, Economic and Political)—rendered into English with Introduction and Notes for the *Sacred Books of the Hindus Series* published by the Panini Office, Allahabad. 2. **Raj Tarangini**—The Annals of Kashmir by the poet-historian Kalhan, rendered into Bengali. 3. **A Socio-Religious Institution of Bengal**—a contribution to the study of Hindu Sociology.

IV. **IN BENGALI :** (i) Historical Essays. (ii) Miscellaneous Essays. (iii) Problems in Modern Education. (iv) Siksha Vijnan or The Science of Education and the Inductive Method of Teaching Series—11 volumes already published, others in preparation.

V. **IN ENGLISH :**—(A) Already Published (*a*) Aids to General Culture Series:—1. Economics. 2. Constitutions. 3. Ancient Europe. 4. Mediæval Europe. 5. English Literature. (*b*) The Man of Letters. (*c*) The Hindu University—what it means. (*d*) The Pedagogy of the Hindus.

(B) **IN PREPARATION :**—1. *Lectures on the Science of History*—An investigation of general principles underlying the course of universal history. 2. *An Introduction to the History of Indian Civilisation*—An attempt to elucidate the working of the forces, both national and international as well as political and non-political, that have moulded the history of the Indian people—based on a study and interpretation of available materials from Biological standpoint. 3. *Studies in Sanskrit Literature*—Literary and Sociological.

by Rai Sarat Chandra Dâs Bahâdur in the memorandum from which extracts have already been given above.

We are glad, therefore, that the Pâṇinî Office has undertaken to publish the Sacred Laws of the Aryas. * * *

For the greater portion of India, Hindu Law is administered according to the Mitakshara School. It is a matter of give regret, that the whole of this authoritative work on Hindu Law has not been translated into English. Since the days of Colebrooke, Indian Lawyers have laid stress on Vyavahâra Adhyâya only. But surely Âchâra and Prâyaśchitta Adhyâyas are as important in deciding questions of Hindu Law as the Vyavahâra Adhyâya.

We wish every success to this new venture of the Paṇini Office and trust that our readers in general and practising lawyers in particular will give every support in their power to this undertaking.

The MODERN REVIEW *writes* :—

The British law-courts in India administer to Hindus their own laws, as laid down in their ancient law-books, in all matters of inheritance and religious and social customs and usage. But many works on Hindu law still remain to be published with translations, after proper editing and collation of readings It is, therefore, of the highest importance, alike to the Government, the Hindu public and the lawyers, that those Sanskrit legal works which are still unpublished and untranslated should be made available for study and reference. In the interests, too, of what may be termed comparative jurisprudence, these laws of the Hindus should be published with translations.

We are glad to find, therefore, that the Pâṇini Office of Allahabad has undertaken to publish "The Sacred Laws of the Aryans." * * * This publishing house has justly acquired fame by its edition of the Ashtâdhyâyi of Pâṇini, of the Siddhanta-Kaumudî, of many philosophical works and of the well-known series of the Sacred Books of the Hindus. * * *

As Mr. Basu is well-known both as a sound Sanskrit scholar and a very able judicial officer, possessed of great legal erudition, the work is sure to be done in an eminently satisfactory manner.

THE
Sacred Laws of the Aryas

Edited by Rai Bahadur Srisa Chandra Vasu.

Professor Jolly in his Tagore Law Lectures says :—

"In modern times, after the establishment of the British rule in India, the hold of the early native institutions over the Indian mind was found to have remained so firm, that it was considered expedient to retain the old national system and adoption amidst the most sweeping changes which had been introduced in the administration of the country and in judicial procedure. It was the desire to ascertain the authentic opinions of the early native legislators in regard to these subjects which led to the discovery of the Sanskrit literature. European Sanskrit philology may be said then to owe a debt of gratitude to the memory of the ancient Sanskrit Lawyers of India."

Sir Henry Sumner Maine says that India

"May yet give us a new science not less valuable than the science of language and folklore. I hesitate to call it comparative jurisprudence, because if it ever exists, its area will be so much wider than the field of law. For India not only contains (or to speak more accurately, did contain) an Aryan language older than any other descendant of the common mother tongue and a variety of names of natural objects less perfectly crystallised than elsewhere into fabulous personages, but it includes a whole world of Aryan institutions, Aryan customs, Aryan laws, Aryan ideas in a far earlier stage of growth and development than any which survive beyond its border."

What Maine hesitated to call comparative jurisprudence cannot be brought into existence unless the legal lore of ancient India is properly studied.

The fact cannot be denied that the contents of the law books of the Hindus are not so well known to Indian legal practitioners unacquainted with Sanskrit as they deserve to be.

To remove this want, the Pâṇini office has undertaken to publish English translations of the Law Books of the Hindus together with their authoritative commentaries.

JUST READY

Yâjñavalkya Smṛiti with the commentary Mitâkṣara, Prâyaśchitta Adhyâya translated into English with copious explanatory notes. Price Ten (10) Rupees.

PANINI OFFICE, BHUVANESWARI ASRAM, BAHADURGANJ, ALLAHABAD.